insight text guide

Virginia Lee

Sunset Boulevard

Dir. Billy Wilder

First published in 2022, reprinted in 2023, 2024, 2025.

Insight Publications Pty Ltd
3/350 Charman Road
Cheltenham VIC 3192
Australia
Tel: +61 3 8571 4950
Email: books@insightpublications.com.au

www.insightpublications.com.au

A catalogue record for this book is available from the National Library of Australia

Billy Wilder's Sunset Boulevard / Virginia Lee

Virginia Lee asserts the moral right to be identified as the author of this work.

ISBNs:
9781922771148 (print)
9781922771155 (digital)

Cover design by Melisa Paredes

Printed by Markono Print Media Pte Ltd

contents

CHARACTER MAP

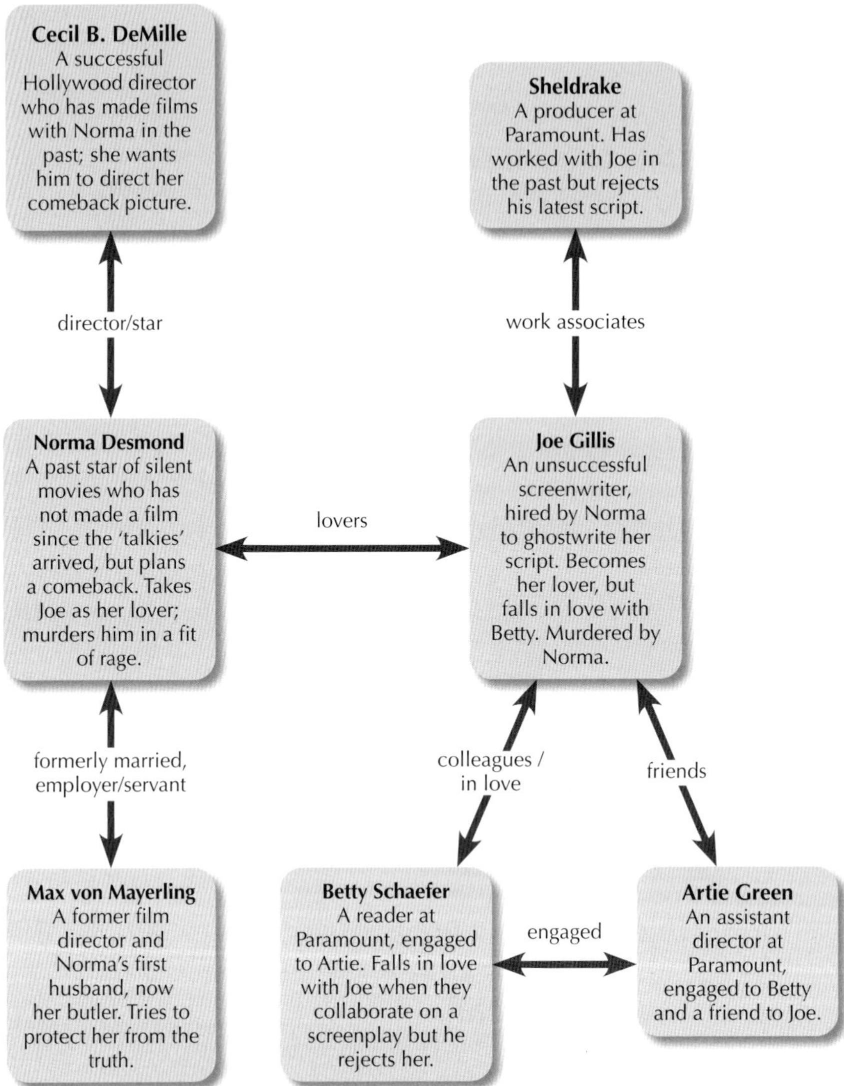

OVERVIEW

About the director

Writer and director Billy Wilder (1906–2002) was one of the most talented and prolific filmmakers in Hollywood. Born in Poland and raised in Vienna, he moved to Berlin in 1926, working as a screenwriter at various film studios before escaping Nazi Germany in 1933. Wilder emigrated to the United States in 1934. He quickly established a name for himself in Hollywood, firstly as a writer then as a director. Among the many honours conferred on Wilder throughout his distinguished career were two Academy Awards for Best Director (out of eight nominations) and three Academy Awards for Best Screenplay / Best Original Screenplay (out of eleven nominations).

With a career that spanned five decades, Wilder's eclectic body of work encompassed a wide variety of genres, from the noir classics *Double Indemnity* (1944) and *The Lost Weekend* (1945) to edgy comedies such as *The Seven Year Itch* (1955), *Some Like It Hot* (1959) and *The Apartment* (1960). As a director, Wilder's primary focus was on the script; he generally eschewed innovative technical devices and showy editing, on the basis that these could distract from the story. Yet, if he was cinematically conservative, Wilder pushed boundaries in his choice of subject matter, challenging many of the social conventions of the 1950s and 1960s.

Wilder enjoyed a long collaborative relationship with writer and producer Charles Brackett. Their partnership was formed in the late 1930s and produced a dozen successful screenplays. *Sunset Boulevard* (1950) was the last project they worked on together. Critically praised and commercially successful at the time of its release, it is regarded as one of Wilder's finest films. It was nominated for eleven Academy Awards and won three for its story and screenplay, musical score, and art direction and set decoration.

Synopsis

A man's body has been discovered floating in the pool of a Hollywood mansion on Sunset Boulevard. Police and press have arrived. Joe Gillis' voice-over then takes us back six months. Joe has come to Hollywood to make a career as a writer, but is having little success. To compound his problems, two representatives from the auto-finance company threaten to repossess his car.

At Paramount Studios, Joe pitches an old rewrite to the producer, Sheldrake. However, the latter rejects the script after his reader, Betty Schaefer, gives it a bad review. Joe then tries to borrow an advance from his agent.

Driving back to Hollywood, Joe is pursued by the finance company reps. When he gets a flat tyre, he eludes them by pulling into the driveway of an apparently deserted mansion on Sunset Boulevard. Mistaken for the expected undertaker, Joe is ushered inside by the butler, Max. Joe recognises the owner of the house as Norma Desmond, a star of the silent screen.

When she discovers that he is a writer, Norma insists that Joe read the script she has written for her comeback film, which she wants Cecil B. DeMille to direct. Seeing an opportunity, Joe wangles himself an editing job. Despite his reservations, he ends up staying the night in a room over the garage. He wakes to find that Norma has had his belongings collected from his apartment and has paid his outstanding rent.

Joe begins work on the script, but it is a laborious process. Norma does not give him money, simply provides his upkeep. The finance company tracks Joe down and tows away his car. Norma resurrects her old Isotta Fraschini (a luxury car) and takes Joe clothes shopping. When the roof of his room over the garage leaks, Joe moves into the main house. He learns that the fan mail Norma receives every week is, in fact, written by Max.

At her New Year's Eve party – where Joe is the only guest – Norma declares that she is in love with him. Repelled by the future she is planning for them both, Joe leaves the palazzo and goes to Artie Green's party. He reconnects with Betty, who is Artie's girlfriend. She has found an old story of Joe's, 'Dark Windows', which she thinks has potential. Joe plans to stay at Artie's, but when he discovers that Norma has attempted suicide, he returns to Sunset Boulevard in alarm. He and Norma become lovers.

Despite Joe's scepticism, Norma sends her completed screenplay to Paramount. By chance, Joe runs into Artie and Betty; the latter informs Joe that she has pitched his story 'Dark Windows' to Sheldrake. Betty urges Joe to work on the script with her, and is angry when he claims that he has given up writing.

Norma receives phone messages from Gordon Cole at Paramount, not from DeMille himself. After a few days, Norma decides to visit DeMille at the studios. He greets her warmly, and she is soon surrounded by actors and crew who remember her from the old days.

Joe takes the opportunity to visit Betty's office nearby, offering her advice on the 'Dark Windows' script. She announces that she and Artie are engaged. When Joe returns to the car, a flustered Max tells him that the calls from Gordon Cole were about renting the Isotta Fraschini for an upcoming film. Emerging from the studio with DeMille, Norma is convinced that her picture will be made and her career will be revived. After the car drives away, DeMille tells his assistant to tell Cole to forget about using Norma's car.

Norma obsessively prepares for her return to the screen. Meanwhile, Joe has been meeting Betty privately at Paramount to collaborate on their screenplay. Their relationship grows with the project. Returning to the house one evening, Joe is challenged by Max, who is 'greatly worried about Madam'. He tells Joe that he was Norma's first husband and directed all her early movies.

Joe and Betty continue to meet, and Betty confesses that she no longer wants to marry Artie. Instead, she has fallen in love with Joe, who reciprocates her feelings. He now defines his entanglement with Norma as a 'nasty mess'.

Beside herself with jealousy, Norma rings Betty to warn her off Joe. Joe calls Norma's bluff, inviting Betty to come over and view his set-up for herself. When she arrives, he breaks off their relationship, leaving her heartbroken. Joe then informs Norma that he is leaving her, telling her *Salome* will never be made and that Max is responsible for her fan mail. Distraught, Norma shoots her lover as he walks away.

The narrative returns to the scene at the start of the film, the morning after the murder. The house is swarming with police and the media. Norma has had a complete mental breakdown and the police cannot make any headway with her. To get her downstairs, Max tells her that they are making a film together. Norma descends the staircase in character, convinced that she is back in the studio playing to the audience that loves her.

Character summaries

Joe Gillis

Joe is the protagonist of *Sunset Boulevard*. About thirty, he is a former reporter from Dayton, Ohio, who is now trying to make it in Hollywood as a screenwriter. He becomes involved with Norma Desmond when he is hired to ghostwrite her screenplay; he then becomes her lover. However, Joe falls in love with Betty Schaefer.

Norma Desmond

The antagonist of the film, Norma is a former star of the silent era who lives in reclusive splendour on Sunset Boulevard. She is fifty and, although she has not made a film for twenty years, she is determined to return to the screen and plans to star in her own screenplay, *Salome*. Norma becomes Joe's lover.

Max von Mayerling

Max, who is about sixty, is Norma's faithful retainer. A former director and Norma's first husband, Max abandoned his career to devote himself to serving the woman he still loves.

Betty Schaefer

Betty is twenty-two and works as a reader at Paramount. She has aspirations to be a writer. She is engaged to Artie, but falls in love with Joe when they work on a screenplay together.

Artie Green

Artie is about thirty, an assistant director at Paramount. He is a good friend of Joe's and engaged to Betty.

Sheldrake

Sheldrake is a successful producer at Paramount Pictures who has worked with Joe in the past. He is about fifty.

Cecil B. DeMille

DeMille is one of the most successful directors in Hollywood. He is about seventy and has been in the industry since its early days. He directed Norma in a number of her silent pictures.

The agent

The agent is a middle-aged man who represents Joe in Hollywood.

BACKGROUND & CONTEXT

The silent film era

The late nineteenth century and early twentieth century saw the global emergence of the film industry, with the silent era reaching its zenith from the early 1910s to the late 1920s. In America, the original studios were located in New York, but the industry quickly centred itself in Hollywood. Silent films did not have recorded sound; title cards on the screen conveyed pivotal moments in the plot. These films were usually accompanied by a pianist or theatre organist.

The early filmmakers were pioneers in this new art form, exploring style and genre, as well as the technical aspects of filmmaking, such as editing, lighting and cinematography. Although filmed in black and white, tinting was used extensively. DW Griffith's *The Birth of a Nation* (1915) is credited with being a landmark production in terms of its scale and technical virtuosity.

Cinema produced stars, many of whom came from a vaudevillian background. Actors such as Rudolph Valentino, Lionel Barrymore, Charlie Chaplin, Mary Pickford and Lillian Gish became household names. Talented Jewish immigrants such as Samuel Goldwyn, William Fox, Louis B. Mayer and the Warner brothers went into production, setting up Hollywood studios.

With technological advances, synchronised dialogue became possible in the late 1920s. In 1927 the first talkie (film with a soundtrack), *The Jazz Singer* starring Al Jolson, was made, sounding the death knell for the silent movie era and the careers of stars who could not make the transition to speaking roles.

Wilder's casting of Gloria Swanson as Norma Desmond was an inspired choice. Swanson's stardom and lifestyle were as prodigious as Norma's. She had not made a successful transition to talkies, but

Sunset Boulevard marked a stunning comeback. Wilder also cast former director Erich von Stroheim – who directed several of Swanson's early films – as Max, and well-known silent screen actors Anna Q Nilsson, HB Warner and Buster Keaton to play the 'waxworks'.

The Golden Age of Hollywood

The period in which *Sunset Boulevard* was made is often called the 'Golden Age of Hollywood'. From the advent of talkies to the early 1960s, the film industry was dominated by the studio system. The major studios – Paramount, Warner Brothers, 20th Century-Fox and Metro-Goldwyn-Mayer (MGM) – employed thousands of actors, directors, writers, technicians and other support staff under contract, thereby controlling their labour and professional practice.

By the mid-1940s, at the height of the industry's popularity, the studios were producing over 400 films a year for worldwide audiences who were hungry for entertainment. On the whole, these films were characterised by a commitment to realism, clearly defined characters, a strong linear plotline – unambiguously resolved – and an increasingly moralistic tone. By the 1960s, though, the studio system was in decline. The influence of foreign films and the emergence of independent production companies, as well as the rise of television, all challenged the big studios' monopoly of the film industry.

Aware of the provocative nature of their screenplay, *Sunset Boulevard* writers Wilder, Charles Brackett and DM Marshman Jr pretended that they were making a comedy in order to circumvent the disapproval of both the censors and studio executives. Their creation – hardly a comedy, except in the most mordant sense – is widely regarded as one of the most superb films to come out of this classic period of Hollywood cinema.

The Production Code

Hollywood both mirrored and reinforced conservative societal standards. From 1930 to 1968, the film industry was regulated by the Production Code, which was initially voluntary and later enforced by an administering body that saw itself as the custodian of public decency. All films produced or exhibited in the United States had to meet the approval of the Production Code Administration (PCA), or distribution would be jeopardised. Anything deemed harmful to public morality – such as nudity, obscene language, overt violence or sexual activity – was prohibited. For example, the fact that Norma and Joe are lovers is never explicitly stated and they have separate bedrooms. Norma towelling down a buffed Joe after his swim is about as suggestive as a scene was allowed to be.

At the same time, *Sunset Boulevard*'s very subject matter, a sexual relationship between an older woman and a much younger man, outside of marriage, was problematic. However, Wilder was a master at skirting around the Production Code and, indeed, enjoyed the challenge. His and Brackett's reputation at Paramount was such that the studio did not require a finished screenplay before going into production. The writers released the script in stages in an attempt to obfuscate its content. By the time *Sunset Boulevard* was scrutinised by the PCA, the picture was already in production. Though some rewriting was required, *Sunset Boulevard* retained its incendiary tone and edgy dialogue.

Given that the Production Code's self-professed rationale was to protect moral values, filmmakers were constrained by its prescriptive 'working principles', which insisted that good and evil be presented in a value-laden way. For characters who transgress the code of ethical behaviour, like Joe and Norma, there must be punitive consequences. Joe's death and Norma's madness play to these expectations.

Film Noir

Film noir refers primarily to a style of filmmaking – the 'look' and tone of a film – rather than a genre. It is a French term, meaning 'black' or 'dark' film, and was first coined by French film critics to describe a particular stable of films that came out of postwar America. These films had their roots in the cinematography of German Expressionism, with its unbalanced compositions and low-key lighting, and drew on the prevailing mood of anxiety, mistrust and pessimism. They were usually, though not exclusively, crime/detective dramas. While the classic noir period in Hollywood was during the 1940s and 1950s, films such as Roman Polanski's *Chinatown* (1974) and Ridley Scott's *Blade Runner* (1982) show the influence of noir.

Noir films explore the underbelly of the human experience, showcasing a bleak, nihilistic world of moral corruption and human fallibility. They typically feature gloomy, oppressive settings; shadowy lighting; cynical, alienated characters who often operate outside the law; and a plot that involves murder, told in flashback and/or narrated by a reflective voice-over. Most noir films of the 1940s and 1950s were shot in black and white, which contributed to the ambience of brooding menace.

America in the 1950s

The characters in *Sunset Boulevard* live in a bubble, their lives rarely intersecting with the outside world. In particular, Norma's reclusive lifestyle means that she seldom leaves the house, let alone Hollywood. However, some points regarding the broader context of the film's milieu are pertinent.

Postwar America had entered into a period of unprecedented economic prosperity. It was a time of fiscal growth – driven by a number of factors including the rapidly developing car industry and a housing boom – increased consumerism and employment opportunities. The film industry was booming despite a repressive political climate. Politically, the 1950s was a deeply conservative decade, dominated by the Cold War and fear of communism. The House Un-American Activities Committee (HUAC) had been established in 1938 to counter the communist 'menace', and after World War II HUAC intensified its efforts to flush out and vilify those viewed as a threat to the American way of life.

The purge that ensued divided and damaged Hollywood: right-wingers testified against friends and colleagues, while directors and actors who were suspected of communist affiliations were targeted by HUAC and blacklisted. Although Wilder is not regarded as a politically driven director, he had experienced Germany under the Nazis and opposed the overreach of HUAC. He was instrumental in creating the 'Committee for the First Amendment', designed to support Hollywood professionals who had been targeted by HUAC. He also refused to endorse the oath of allegiance proposed by the Screen Directors Guild.

In the 1950s, gender roles were clearly delineated; women of this generation were largely dependent on men, economically and socially. Although Hollywood was one of the few contexts in which women, even if married, could have independent careers, all of the power structures in the film are invested in men. Nothing more clearly illustrates this male-dominated hierarchy than the chain of command through which Norma's message is passed on to DeMille at Paramount.

GENRE, STRUCTURE & LANGUAGE

Genre

Billy Wilder's film noir about an ageing actress who wants to reclaim her stardom has become one of the enduring cinema classics. *Sunset Boulevard* is a hard-hitting, insightful exposé of Hollywood's underbelly – a disturbing indictment of the film industry that forensically lays open its pretentions and illusions. The text features many noir conventions: a bleak tone; dark, moody cinematography; a narrative involving murder, presented in flashback; and a disillusioned hero. Norma Desmond is a classic example of the femme fatale: mysterious, predatory and duplicitous.

Sunset Boulevard also blends romance, allegory and black comedy. The Boulevard becomes a metaphor for Hollywood itself: desirable and alluring, but dangerous. In keeping with the didactic expectations of the times, Joe and Norma's fates highlight the pitfalls of fame, and the ease with which ambition and celebrity can corrupt.

There are potentially three romantic triangles in *Sunset Boulevard*, all of which are resolved by Joe's death. The exploitative nature of Joe and Norma's relationship is juxtaposed against Max's selfless devotion; similarly, the opportunism it represents is implicitly compared to Betty's innocence. Artie's love, legitimised by his marriage proposal, is set in opposition to the conflicted love that Joe offers Betty.

Finally, Brackett and Wilder's screenplay is, at times, extremely funny. The humour is cynical and character-driven, often arising from the contrast between Norma's delusional assumptions and Joe's wry responses. When the actress announces that, having read her horoscope in detail, Norma's astrologer advises sending *Salome* to DeMille, Joe asks, 'Did she read the script?'

Structure

Sunset Boulevard has a circular structure, within which the narrative follows a linear trajectory. The film commences with the discovery of Joe Gillis' body floating in the pool of a mansion on Sunset Boulevard. An extended flashback then takes the audience back six months to 'the day when it all started'. We follow Joe's fraught relationship with silent screen star Norma Desmond as she plans her comeback to the screen, before returning full circle to the morning after his murder. This structure enables us to retrospectively view Joe and Norma's story. The film concludes with a short coda, or postscript, that delineates Norma's fate.

The plot is structured according to the classic Hollywood crime format: an exposition, followed by complications that cause tensions to rise to a climax, then a denouement and resolution. Like all crime stories, the narrative framework subverts cause and effect in that it commences with Joe's murder. This structure creates mystery and heightens dramatic tension. Interwoven with the main plotline of Norma's decline is the love affair of Joe and Betty – the narrative device that triggers Joe's murder.

Language

Wilder and Brackett's clever, acerbic script features fast-paced dialogue, mordant wit, sharp observational humour and some memorable one-liners.

Daringly, *Sunset Boulevard* is narrated by a corpse. Joe Gillis' voice-over anchors the film, establishing its dry, satirical tone from the outset. Commentating on the aftermath of his own murder is a bizarre parody of Joe's previous life as a reporter, and indicative of the black humour that runs through the film. Joe's voice is cynical in the extreme. After spending too long in Hollywood, for too little reward, he has few illusions left. His default facetious humour is designed to diffuse tension and/or extricate himself from awkward situations.

The use of a voice-over means that there is a direct line of communication from Joe to the audience: 'Let's go back about six months.' Inevitably, by presenting events from Joe's point of view, Wilder invites sympathy for his protagonist, despite his many flaws and his own cumulative self-contempt. Joe, of course, has the advantage of hindsight. Retrospectively, he can see exactly where he went wrong, and this awareness is a feature of the narrative: 'Maybe I'd been an idiot not to have sensed it was coming.'

Joe's deadpan irony is regularly set against Norma's extremely literal mindset. When he asks, straight-faced, if Norma is planning to play the sixteen-year-old Salome, she replies with characteristic hauteur, 'Who else?' Joe and Betty also bounce off each other like ping-pong balls. At their first prickly meeting, Betty tries to soften her criticism of his screenplay, *Bases Loaded*, with self-effacing humour: 'Right now I wish I could crawl in a hole and pull it in after me.' To which Joe responds through gritted teeth, 'If I could be of any help …'

Not surprisingly, Norma delivers some of the most unforgettable lines. Her classic retort – 'I *am* big. It's the pictures that got small' – has become inextricably associated with the character, encapsulating the former star's pride and myopia in one brilliant masterstroke.

Intertextuality

Intertextuality is a feature of *Sunset Boulevard*, with a number of other texts being referenced throughout. These allusions link back to the characters or the themes, providing an artful commentary on the interaction taking place. For example, when Joe first arrives at Norma's palazzo, it reminds him of Miss Havisham's house in Charles Dickens' novel, *Great Expectations*. Joe wonders if Norma, like the vindictive Miss Havisham, has been 'taking it out on the world because she'd been given the go-by'. Dickens' protagonist, Pip, is deceived into thinking that Miss Havisham is the benefactor who rescues him from extreme poverty, and while Norma actually does save Joe financially, she also manipulates him and takes advantage of his reliance on her. Their relationships with these older women expose both Pip's and Joe's self-deception and dubious priorities.

Much later, Joe is reading Irwin Shaw's *The Young Lions*, a 1948 novel that explores the ethical struggle of three young men during wartime, and the ways in which they can be corrupted by false beliefs. The reference to this narrative, by implication, critiques the questionable values promoted by Hollywood.

The shadow of the biblical story *Salome* hovers over *Sunset Boulevard*. In summarising the plot of her screenplay for Joe, Norma foreshadows his murder: 'He [John the Baptist] rejects her so she demands his head on a golden tray.' Perhaps it is no accident that DeMille is filming the epic *Samson and Delilah* when Norma visits Paramount – a text that also portrays a woman emasculating a man.

The film's title

Sunset Boulevard is a major thoroughfare that runs from the centre of downtown Los Angeles to the Pacific coast, cutting through West Hollywood, Beverly Hills and Bel Air. The 1920s saw the extension of the western stretch of road and the development of the area known as the 'Riviera section' because of its proximity to the coast. Norma's 'grim Sunset castle' is located further back towards Hollywood in the Holmby Hills.

In the text, Sunset Boulevard is almost a character in its own right – wealthy, exclusive, intimidating. The road is long, with many twists and turns, not easily navigated, nor easily accessible. It represents success, but also peril – much like Hollywood itself. Joe initially sees 10086 Sunset Boulevard (Norma's address) as an escape, but increasingly recognises that it is a prison. Finally, it becomes a death sentence.

Elements of film style

While characters, themes and values are common to all narrative texts, there are also features specific to cinema. Any analysis of *Sunset Boulevard* should use the correct metalanguage and discuss the elements that characterise this form.

Actors and acting

Sunset Boulevard pivots around a small cast of only four main characters. Gloria Swanson dominates the picture as the ageing movie queen, capturing the extremes of Norma Desmond's volatile personality, from outrageous to vulnerable. Swanson's performance appropriates the facial contortions and histrionic mannerisms of the silent movie actor. In her personal interactions, Norma uses the same big gestures and exaggerated expressions that she deployed on the screen.

By contrast, William Holden's character, Joe Gillis, is very aware of his limitations. Holden's understated delivery and self-deprecating humour provide the foil to Norma's histrionics. In spite of Joe's blind spots and ethical flaws, he never entirely loses the sympathy of the audience. These two leads are ably supported by Erich von Stroheim – who, carrying himself with stiff, unsmiling restraint, brings dignity to the role of Max – and Nancy Olson, as Joe's youthful love interest.

Mise en scène

Mise en scène refers to the visual and design elements of a film. Everything we see in the frame – sets, locations, costumes and lighting – has been deliberately selected and is encoded with meaning. Setting can provide information about the characters and their circumstance; background details can be an ironic comment on events taking place in the foreground.

Norma's Italianate mansion, with its overdecorated interiors, is a shrine that reveals much about its owner's disconnection from reality and obsession with the past. The baroque grandeur of the house – eight master bedrooms, a sunken tub in every bathroom, a bowling alley and a home movie theatre – trumpets wealth with an ostentation that was once fashionable. Now, the palazzo is 'a great big white elephant of a place', cluttered with memorabilia from a past life. The many framed photographs and portraits of the actress in her prime highlight Norma's narcissism, as well as her desperate desire to turn back the clock.

In a similar way, costumes help define the characters. The wardrobe that costume designer Edith Head designed for Gloria Swanson expresses Norma's penchant for the dramatic. Even when she is home alone, Norma's clothes ooze theatricality; when Joe first meets her, she is wearing a floor-length dress with leopard trim, a matching leopard turban, dark glasses and heavy bracelets. Although Norma's sartorial choices reference contemporary design, they also seem slightly out of touch.

By contrast, Max is a conservative figure. His uniform of a formal black suit and white gloves reveals little except the seriousness with which he takes his role. Joe's wardrobe fluctuates with his fortunes. He is not someone who cares much about what he wears, but Norma disapproves of his 'filling-station' shirt and 'baggy pants'. Joe's kept status is advertised through the expensive clothes and jewellery that his lover provides.

Cinematography

The great strength of Wilder's pictures lies in their clever dialogue and memorable characterisations; he never wanted the cinematography to overshadow the writing. Nevertheless *Sunset Boulevard* contains many striking images, filmed in classic noir style. For example, as police cars speed towards the murder scene, Los Angeles' famous palm trees are silhouetted against the dawn sky in a shot that is both beautiful and sinister.

The black-and-white cinematography exploits the interplay between light and dark that runs through the film – a dichotomy that relates back to the characters themselves and the noir themes explored. The drama of Max's revelation of his past relationship with Norma is matched by the dark lighting of the scene. Similarly, the ongoing tension between illusion and reality is emphasised by stark contrasts in setting. The oppressive, shadowy interiors of Norma's mansion are juxtaposed with scenes shot outside in the bright Los Angeles sunlight – by the pool, or driving around the city – throwing Norma's agoraphobic lifestyle and her oddities into even sharper relief.

Wilder uses a dissolve to connect most of the scenes in *Sunset Boulevard*, a popular editing technique at the time. These dissolves may indicate a significant time lapse, such as the slow dissolve that takes us back six months at the beginning of the film. Sometimes they emphasise a more meaningful connection – for example, the burgeoning relationship between Joe and Betty.

Sound

Franz Waxman's moody, eclectic score sets the tone of *Sunset Boulevard*; the opening three chords immediately signal drama and emotional tension. The music encompasses a great range, from the sinister chords that accompany dramatic moments in the script, to the breezy dance pieces of New Year's Eve. The plaintive leitmotiv (theme) associated with Norma, with its tango overtones, is first heard when she is initially seen on the balcony. It has morphed into a more tortured version by the end of the film when Norma descends the staircase, lost in madness.

In addition to Waxman's original score, music is used as a diegetic element within the world of the text to reflect the emotional mood of particular characters or situations. For example, when it becomes clear that Joe's presence at the palazzo will be ongoing, Max's organ-playing reaches a furious crescendo. His rendition of Bach's *Toccata and Fugue in D Minor* suggests that he is less than happy about the arrangement, while the piece's associations with the horror genre foreshadow the tragedy to come. Conversely, the piano duet, 'Buttons and Bows', reflects the carefree, youthful atmosphere of Artie's party. The same evening, 'Auld Lang Syne' is played after Norma's suicide attempt, ironically greeting Joe and Norma's forthcoming New Year.

SCENE-BY-SCENE ANALYSIS

Chapter divisions used in this section are those in the DVD of *Sunset Boulevard*. The time codes given here are approximate, as these can vary depending on the device and software used to play the DVD.

Chapter 1: The Corpse (0:00:00)

Summary: *Opening credits; a body is discovered in the pool of a Hollywood mansion.*

Menacing chords announce the beginning of the film as the camera slowly tracks down to the street kerb where the title, written as *Sunset Blvd*, is stencilled. The camera pulls back, travelling across and up the boulevard while the opening credits appear on the screen. The insistent, percussive score conveys both drama and urgency. Finally, a long shot shows the whole road and, in the distance, the headlights of approaching vehicles.

It is 5 am and the light is muted. Police converge on a mansion on Sunset Boulevard and we learn that a sensational story is about to break; an old-time movie star is involved, 'one of the biggest'.

At first, it is not clear that Joe Gillis is the murder victim. The camera simply shows a man's corpse floating face down in the pool while the voice-over explains in the third person that, although the 'poor dope' always wanted a pool, the price 'turned out to be a little high'. Wilder plays with our expectations here. Although Joe's identity is revealed when we see the dead man's face, the scene demands close attention from its audience – after all, the narrator is unlikely to be a dead man. For the difficult 'fish's view' shot, Wilder and the cinematographer placed a mirror on the bottom of the pool and filmed the reflection. Joe's body is viewed from underneath, while the blurred images of police and press, hovering by the side of the pool, look down at the scene.

Q What does the voice-over tell us about the narrator?

Chapter 2: Money Trouble (0:02:38)

Summary: *The finance company threatens to repossess Joe's car; Joe tries, unsuccessfully, to sell a script to Paramount.*

A slow dissolve into a streetscape takes the audience back six months. Joe is introduced when the camera pans across to his building and through the open window of his small, unkempt apartment. The voice-over informs us that things are 'tough' at the moment, signposted by the unmade bed that doubles as Joe's desk, the full ashtray, his unshaven appearance and the fact that he is still in his bathrobe in the middle of the day. Joe's flippant tone to the finance company reps – 'You say the cutest things' – is at odds with his harassed body language once they leave.

Paramount Studios' entrance gates feature prominently in the film. They are the literal and figurative gateway to a world of success and creativity – a world from which Joe is currently excluded. Hollywood sets a frenetic pace, and time is money. Accordingly, Joe's pitch of *Bases Loaded* to Sheldrake is delivered with rapid-fire economy. Unfortunately, his plot is so predictable that the producer anticipates its ending. Betty Schaefer's damning appraisal of *Bases Loaded* – 'I wouldn't bother. It's from hunger' – is the final nail in Joe's coffin.

Key vocabulary

20th Century-Fox: one of the biggest Hollywood studios.

Alan Ladd: well-known Hollywood actor, contracted to Paramount.

Darryl F. Zanuck: American film producer, and the studio head of Fox from 1944 until 1956.

Mocambo-Romanoff rut: refers to celebrity haunt Mocambo, a nightclub on Sunset Boulevard, and Michael Romanoff, a well-known Hollywood restaurateur.

Q What are your first impressions of Joe Gillis?

Q Discuss the significance of Schwab's Pharmacy.

Chapter 3: A White Elephant of a House (0:09:55)

Summary: *Joe is pursued by the finance company reps; he eludes them by pulling into the driveway of an apparently deserted mansion on Sunset Boulevard.*

Driving back to Hollywood, Joe mulls over his options; returning to the mundane life of a small-town reporter seems increasingly likely. Like an ominous finger of fate, the signpost in the foreground points Joe toward Sunset Boulevard.

During the tense car chase that follows, the syncopated rhythms of the score – an urgent exchange between brass and percussion – convey Joe's desperation. The camera follows the speeding cars as they lurch around the Boulevard's winding hills, until a tyre blowout forces Joe to pull into an unknown driveway.

The stillness that surrounds the palazzo, and the sense of time arrested, presents a marked contrast to the frantic pace of the pursuit. The house has seen better days; its air of decay reminds Joe of Miss Havisham's house in *Great Expectations*. Joe also notes that 'a neglected house gets an unhappy look. This one had it in spades', an observation that pre-empts the dark psychology of its occupant.

Q Discuss Joe's plan 'to stash the car'. What does it reveal about him?

Chapter 4: 'I am big. It's the pictures that got small.' (0:12:55)

Summary: *Joe is mistaken for the undertaker; he meets Norma for the first time and recognises her as a great star of the silent screen.*

Joe hears Norma hail him imperiously before he sees her. As the camera zooms slowly in, the impression is of a solitary, enigmatic figure. Norma is standing alone at the window, framed by the columns on the balcony of her palazzo and half-obscured by the blinds. She is also wearing dark glasses – an odd choice inside. The low-angle shot reinforces her aloof presence and foreshadows the control she will wield in the coming relationship.

The interior of the palazzo is flamboyant in the extreme. In particular, Norma's bedroom, festooned with an excessive number of cushions and ruffles, demonstrates a triumph of extravagance over taste. The camera follows Joe's eyes as he doubtfully takes in the decor. The unexpected sight of a small body, draped with a shawl, adds to the macabre atmosphere.

It is only when Norma removes her dark glasses that Joe recognises the former star. Norma's diatribe against the advent of talkies reveals her contempt and frustration; retirement has been forced on her. When the actress insists that she is still 'big' – 'It's the pictures that got small' – her face in close-up fills the frame. Norma takes Joe's defence that he is 'just a writer' personally: 'You've made a rope of words and strangled this business.'

Key point

In spite of their apparent differences, Joe and Norma do have one thing in common. Both have been dismissed by Hollywood as having outlived their usefulness.

Key vocabulary

Douglas Fairbanks: American actor of the silent era, famous for his swashbuckling roles.

John Gilbert: American actor of the silent era.

Rudolph Valentino: one of the biggest stars of the 1920s; known as 'The Latin Lover'.

Q What are your first impressions of Norma Desmond?

Chapter 5: The Salome Script (0:17:04)

Summary: *Norma asks Joe to read her script; Joe wangles himself a job.*

Norma frames her comeback as a public service to cinema: 'A return to the millions of people who've never forgiven me for deserting the screen.' Paradoxically, despite her disgust at sound destroying silent movies, she has written a screenplay.

Scripts are a central motif in the text. Joe's own efforts have become clichéd and stale. By contrast, *Salome* is so bizarrely long it could be 'six important pictures'. Joe's misgivings about its merit are confirmed as he ploughs through the 'silly hodgepodge of melodramatic plots'. Norma's anxiety is evident as Joe reads the screenplay. She watches him closely, her hand clutching the back of the chair, 'coiled up like a watch spring'. From Joe's perspective, the only thing that alleviates the tension is the arrival of the undertaker to remove the tiny corpse – Norma's pet chimpanzee – which Joe ironically describes as 'comedy relief'.

Subsequently, Norma's confidence reasserts itself. Her posture becomes more relaxed, and there is even a hint of flirtation when she widens her eyes at the end of the scene. The slow pan to a close-up of Norma's face as she apparently innocuously suggests that Joe stay the night, accompanied by the brooding soundtrack, intimates that the arrangement will not be as straightforward as it seems. A photo of the young Norma also comes into the frame, a reminder of the ephemeral nature of celebrity and the inevitable passing of time.

Q What is the difference between a 'comeback' and a 'return'?

Q Comment on the mise en scène in Norma's salon.

Chapter 6: An Invitation to Stay (0:23:01)

Summary: *Joe spends the night in the room over the garage; Norma has Joe's belongings collected from his apartment.*

Even though he has been manoeuvred into staying the night, Joe still thinks he is in control of the situation. He is content to humour his strange hosts, observing that 'the whole place seemed to have been stricken with a kind of creeping paralysis, out of beat with the rest of the world, crumbling apart in slow motion'. Joe's reflection on the former glory of the palazzo and its occupants – including the stars who swam in Norma's pool '10 000 midnights ago' – throws its current neglect into sharp relief. The pool is emblematic of success – a coveted status symbol. However, Norma's pool is currently dry and hosting a family of rats.

Joe's face is in close-up, framed by the parallel lines of the blind and open window, as he watches the bizarre ceremony of the chimpanzee's last rites. The scene exposes the emptiness of Norma's life; it was 'as if she were laying to rest an only child'.

By the end of the chapter, Joe is beginning to understand that the actress has the upper hand. He loses the advantage when she becomes aware of his financial stress and he unwillingly complies with her demands.

Key point

Joe's nightmare, where 'a chimp was dancing for pennies', foreshadows his own fate – replacing the chimpanzee as Norma's cossetted companion.

Key vocabulary

Mabel Normand: American silent-film actress who was implicated in the murder of her lover, William Desmond Taylor.

Q Why does Norma cover Joe's unpaid rent?

Q How else does the filmmaker suggest that Norma is the one in control?

Chapter 7: The Face of a Star (0:28:04)

Summary: *Joe works on the script; Joe and Norma watch a film together.*

Joe's voice-over details the unexpected complications of his new job, while the camera zooms slowly into a mid-shot of him sitting at the desk. Joe soon discovers that Norma is 'plain crazy' regarding her celluloid identity, and the script is simply an expression of this narcissism. Any attempt to edit her 'precious brainchild' is met with fierce resistance. The camera's slow pan across the many images of 'Norma Desmond' that surround them reinforces the actress' absolute focus on self. Wherever he is in the palazzo, Joe is under scrutiny, his every move observed by these watching, knowing eyes.

Wilder again blurs the lines between fact and fiction. Just as the photos in Norma's salon are actually those of a young Gloria Swanson, Wilder uses footage from *Queen Kelly* (1928), an old Swanson movie, written and directed by Erich von Stroheim.

A dramatic low-angle shot accompanies Norma's outburst over the current crop of 'idiot producers'. Jumping to her feet, she gestures at the screen, while light from the projector surrounds the back of her head like a halo. She then turns her head imperiously, so that the light hits her profile, as she vows to show them 'what a star looks like'. Though the overall effect is one of conviction and authority, there is also an element of irony. Clearly Norma no longer dominates the film industry and is unlikely to ever do so again.

Key vocabulary

Greta Garbo: one of the greatest stars of the 1930s who famously retired at the height of her fame.

Q Comment on the clothes that Norma wears.

Q Is Norma just being 'a fan' when she clutches Joe's arm during the film? How else might you interpret the gesture?

Chapter 8: Bridge with the Wax Works (0:31:47)

Summary: *Joe loses his car to the finance company; Norma resurrects the Isotta Fraschini and takes Joe shopping.*

The only company that Norma tolerates at the palazzo are 'the waxworks'. Like her, they are former actors, 'dim figures you may still remember from the silent days'. They watch the interplay between Joe and Norma impassively, although the two men exchange a knowing look when the couple argues. They assume that Norma has already taken Joe as her lover and, indeed, his role is morphing into that of a kept man: 'Empty the ashtray will you, Joe, dear.'

Joe's request for money falls on deaf ears. Norma trivialises his concern as he watches his car being towed away, insisting that 'we' don't need another car. Joe is becoming increasingly impotent, financially, and now physically, reliant on Norma's largesse.

Key point

Little by little, Joe relinquishes his independence, and by the time he allows Norma to buy him an expensive wardrobe, he is significantly compromised. The close-up of the shop assistant leering into Joe's face – 'Well as long as the lady's paying for it, why not take the vicuña' – highlights the ethical dilemma that has crept up on Joe.

Key vocabulary

Vicuña: a soft, delicate woollen fabric (a vicuña is a South American ruminant, a hoofed herbivorous grazing mammal).

Q Discuss the idea that if Joe was truly ambitious, he would not have 'sold out' to Norma so easily.

Chapter 9: The Husbands' Bedroom (0:36:10)

Summary: *Joe moves into the main house.*

In Hollywood, everything borders on the extreme; even the rain is oversized. Being moved into 'the room of the husbands' foreshadows Joe's romantic involvement with Norma. At this point, it is easier for Joe to feel sorry for his hostess and see his sojourn at the palazzo as a distraction from the real world, than to examine her motives and the worrying implications of the arrangement. The twin discoveries that Norma suffers from depression and that Max writes her fan mail reveal to Joe, and the audience, the extent to which the former star is living in a world of fantasy.

Wilder draws our attention to the mise en scène in Norma's bedroom. The bed, featuring drapes and a carved Cupid, is shaped 'like a gilded rowboat'. Overall, the room is 'the perfect setting for a silent movie queen' and for playing out Norma's fantasies.

Chapter 10: New Year's Eve (0:39:31)

Summary: *Norma declares her love for Joe; in response, Joe escapes to Artie's New Year's Eve party, but returns to the palazzo after Norma attempts suicide.*

Norma's 'sad and embarrassing revelation' on New Year's Eve brings the situation to a head. On the dance floor, she does her own version of Salome's dance of the seven veils. The lack of other guests, Norma's flirtatious manner and her plans for their future all point to her emotional investment in the relationship. The gold cigarette case, with its revealing inscription, is a tangible emblem of Norma's regard for Joe. It is also a symbol of her wealth and her underlying assumption that she can buy whatever she wants, including a lover.

Max watches their subsequent altercation from the sidelines with an inscrutable expression as the band plays on. When Joe leaves the palazzo, his watch chain becomes caught on the lock of the gate, suggesting that it will not be easy for him to extricate himself from the web in which he is entangled. The image of Joe hitchhiking in the pouring rain is a sobering contrast to the sumptuous surrounds he has just left, and underlines the choice he is making.

Artie's noisy, crowded apartment is a world away from the formal, empty dance floor of Norma's palazzo. In his white tie and tails, Joe stands out like the proverbial sore thumb. Desperate to put the evening with Norma behind him, Joe happily slips into flirtatious mode with Betty. However, the news that Norma has cut her wrists with his razor sees Joe leave the party in a panic.

Norma may well have 'great pride', but she is not averse to using emotional blackmail and misrepresenting herself as a helpless victim to get what she wants. She plays on Joe's sense of remorse and guilt, threatening further suicide attempts. When it becomes clear that he will stay with her, Norma's long-fingered hands, nails like talons, grasp his lapel, drawing his head down towards hers with single-minded intent. The accompanying soundtrack reinforces the ominous impression that this romance will not have a happy ending.

Key point

Returning to the palazzo is a critical turning point for Joe. In choosing to become Norma's lover, he is turning his back on his previous life and isolating himself from his peers. Even more importantly, he loses agency.

Key vocabulary

Adolphe Menjou: American actor of the 1920s and 1930s who was known for his dapper dress style.

Q Describe New Year's Eve from Max's perspective. What do he and Joe have in common?

Q Discuss Joe's motives in giving in to Norma.

Chapter 11: A Kept Man (0:53:50)

Summary: *Betty is trying to track down Joe but Max rejects her phone calls; Norma sends her script to Paramount; Joe bumps into Artie and Betty; Betty urges him to work on 'Dark Windows' with her.*

Norma towels Joe down when he emerges from the renovated swimming pool, signalling a fresh start and a new intimacy in their relationship. Norma is glowing, basking in the pleasure that a new romance brings. She is intractable about her script, which she sends to DeMille based on her horoscope. In vain, Joe tries to diffuse her enthusiasm: 'I hope you realise, Norma, that scripts don't sell on astrologers' charts.'

Going out to a bridge game is one of several times that Wilder films Joe and Norma together in the back seat of the Isotta Fraschini. In each case, there is an obvious disconnect between the pair. Although they are positioned side by side in the frame, Joe's body language suggests boredom and indifference, rather than intimacy. Norma's casual gesture when she gives Joe money for the cigarettes *he* has offered to buy emphasises her assumption that she will pay for everything.

Q What do we learn about Betty in this chapter?

Q Given the constraints imposed by the Production Code, how does Wilder convey the fact that Joe and Norma are sleeping together?

Chapter 12: The Norma Desmond Follies (0:58:38)

Summary: *Norma entertains Joe; she receives a call from Paramount.*

Whenever Norma suspects that Joe's interest is waning, she performs 'the Norma Desmond Follies'. Her impersonation of Charlie Chaplain's iconic 'little tramp' reveals her to be a gifted comic, and is one of the few times she is not taking herself too seriously.

The twirling parasol with which Norma introduces her routine is a pointed reminder that time is passing while Joe wastes his talent and energy lounging on the actress' couch. He is being sucked down into a vortex, and the contrast between what he was when he first arrived in Hollywood – ambitious and hungry – and what he has now become, is stark.

While Joe's life is now characterised by inertia, a tedious daily round of passively acquiescing to Norma's whims, she is energised by the relationship. Unusually cheerful, indulgent and funny, she does everything possible to keep her lover engaged.

Key vocabulary

Charlie Chaplin: actor, director, producer, writer and composer, Chaplin was one of the greatest stars of early twentieth-century cinema.

Sennett Bathing Beauties: an act set up by comedy producer Mack Sennett in 1915, featuring a chorus line of young women in bathing suits.

Chapter 13: Parading to Paramount (1:01:24)

Summary: *Norma visits Paramount Studios.*

Norma's impatience inevitably overcomes her pride, and after three days she is 'good and ready' to speak to DeMille. The visit to Paramount highlights the cruel disparity between past and present. When Max tells the official on the gate that no appointment is necessary as he's bringing Norma Desmond, the response is 'Norma who?' The name is unfamiliar to most under the age of forty.

Norma's car underlines the position she is in. The handmade $28 000 Isotta Fraschini was once a symbol of her wealth and luxurious lifestyle. Now it is a relic, much like its owner, reduced to a potential prop in a movie. Max sitting stiffly at the wheel creates an even more anachronistic image.

Chapter 14: A Meeting with Mr. DeMille (1:04:42)

Summary: *Norma speaks to DeMille; Joe catches up with Betty.*

DeMille is shooting *Samson and Delilah*, the 1949 biblical epic that he had just completed in real life. The high-angle shot of Stage 18 shows it to be a hive of organised chaos – the frame encompasses the whole set, cameras, lights, extras and technicians. A pulsating light globe in the foreground adds to the energy. Behind the scenes, extras smoking in biblical costume as they wait for their cue present a droll image.

Tellingly, when Norma is seated in DeMille's chair, she pushes away the microphone – that hated symbol of her redundancy – in irritation. Hog-eye shines the spotlight on the actress and the high-angle shot has the simultaneous effect of emphasising her former status as a great star, even as it underlines her current insignificance. Norma is soon surrounded by extras and technicians. Her manner implies that she accepts their adulation as her due; in reality, she is deeply moved: 'I had no idea how much I'd missed it.' Nevertheless, there is a flash of the old hauteur: 'And remember, darling, I don't work before 10 in the morning and never after 4.30 in the afternoon.' It clearly does not occur to Norma that she is not still in a position to dictate terms.

Despite his discomfort at their previous fractious parting, Joe tries hard to charm his way back into Betty's good graces. Wilder uses close-ups as the pair throw around ideas, hinting at their (as yet unacknowledged) attraction to each other. By the time Joe leaves, the relationship has regained its playful, flirtatious footing, with Betty's light-hearted threat to throw her half-eaten apple at him.

Q What do we learn about Max from this chapter?

Q Comment on Joe's body language in the scene with Betty. What does it reveal?

Chapter 15: Joe Sneaks Out (1:12:48)

Summary: *Norma prepares for her return; Joe meets Betty at Paramount to work on their script.*

Joe's voice-over accompanies the montage of Norma's punishing beauty regime, showing her elaborate efforts to be camera-ready. The music conveys her sense of urgency. She is focused and single-minded, 'like an athlete training for the Olympic Games'.

Meanwhile, Joe has an agenda of his own, going out at night to work with Betty after Norma has gone to bed. During their scene together, Norma switches gears from suspicious, to needy, to dominating. In spite of the incongruity of her ridiculous chin strap and face patches, the low-angle shot as she challenges her lover reinforces the power she wields in their relationship. So, too, does the possessive running of her hand through Joe's hair as she asserts, 'Of course you haven't [done anything wrong] – I wouldn't let you.'

When we first observe Joe and Betty collaborating on their screenplay, they are silhouetted against the two windows of Betty's little office, in separate frames within the frame. The scene hums with purpose and energy. Once the camera moves inside, their enjoyment of each other's company is obvious. This new script represents a future for Joe, morphing from an image of defeat into a symbol of hope.

As Betty looks for a cigarette, the camera zooms slowly into a close-up of the gold cigarette case with its incriminating inscription, 'Mad about the Boy'. The shot draws attention to Betty's scrutiny while also reminding the audience of Joe's dependency on Norma and the complexity of pursuing another relationship. A sheepish Joe gives Betty a heavily edited version of the truth of his situation.

Q During their conversation, both Joe and Norma use emotional appeals. What are they? To what extent are they effective?

Q Discuss the irony in Joe's statement: 'That's the trouble with you readers, you know all the plots.'

Chapter 16: Untitled Love Story (1:17:56)

Summary: *Joe and Betty's friendship grows; Joe confronts Max; Norma is jealous; Joe and Betty declare their love.*

Wilder uses another dissolve to connect this scene with the previous one. Joe and Betty are seen walking companionably through the deserted lot and, throughout the scene, Wilder charts their growing intimacy. The camera moves from one to the other, until we finally see them together in the frame. The close-up of Joe kissing Betty's nose – half in jest, half in earnest – brings home the dangerous game they are playing. Betty's youth and desirability inevitably invite a comparison with Norma. To Joe, his colleague's hair smells like 'freshly laundered linen handkerchiefs'; by contrast, Norma uses a scent that reminds him of tuberose flowers – an odour he finds cloying and unattractive.

Returning to the palazzo, Joe encounters Max, waiting in the shadows. The dim lighting adds to the menacing atmosphere. In the confrontation that follows, Joe is filmed from below. Working on his own script has given him back some dignity; moreover, when he urges Max to be honest with Norma, his words carry moral authority. However, Max sees it as his mission to protect his delusional employer from the truth. The startling revelation that not only did he direct Norma's early pictures, he was also her first husband, speaks of his obsessive devotion. Close-ups convey the intensity of Max's feeling.

Back at Paramount, Joe's guilt makes him assume that Betty's unhappy preoccupation is due to her hearing rumours about his living arrangements through Hollywood's small-town gossip. Falling in love was not part of his, or Betty's, plan.

Q Why does Norma imagine the worst?

Q Discuss the camera angles and the framing in the last scene between Joe and Betty.

Chapter 17: Betty's Exit (1:26:19)

Summary: *Norma rings Betty; Joe invites Betty over and explains his set-up with Norma; he breaks up with Betty.*

The high-angle shot as Joe opens the gate to his 'peculiar prison' emphasises his difficult situation. However, throughout the subsequent confrontation Joe is filmed from below, signifying a shift in the power balance. He is unmoved by Norma's histrionics and empowered by his own decision to be honest. Uncharacteristically, he throws Norma off guard by using silence as a weapon.

In this chapter, soundtrack and cinematography work together to build tension. For example, as Betty and Connie (her roommate) speed towards their unknown destination, their faces in luminous close-up present a striking contrast to the darkness that surrounds them, in classic noir style. Betty's anxiety is palpable. When she arrives at the gloomy palazzo, her first words to Joe are 'I don't know why I'm so scared'.

As Joe circles the salon, explaining his ostensibly 'simple set-up', the camera follows him, panning across the cluttered mise en scène as if to emphasise Norma's eccentricities. The self-contempt with which Joe explains he cannot leave his many 'things' is unmistakable. Conscious of Norma listening upstairs, Joe is as deliberately offensive as possible; his patronising 'Look sweetie, be practical' is designed to alienate Betty.

Again, the pool is presented as the quintessential symbol of success. Inviting Betty to bring Artie over for a swim, Joe switches on the pool lights. The sharply delineated rectangle, glowing in the night, is supposedly too desirable to forgo. Betty is a heartbroken but dignified figure as she leaves the palazzo. She gives Joe one last look before running to the car, leaving him framed by the gates, grief etched on his face. Another low-angle shot positions us to view Joe's decision as heroic – even if his previous conduct has not been. The camera tilts upwards to reveal Norma watching avidly from the gallery above.

Key point

Until now, Joe has been studiously avoiding the facts. He realises belatedly that relationships carry responsibilities – 'There it was. Betty Schaefer's future in the palm of my hand' – and finds it impossible to reconcile his love for her with his affair with Norma. He feels that he has forfeited the right to love.

Q What does Norma's slur, 'men of his sort', tell us?

Q Joe is still not being completely honest with Betty. Is he making another mistake?

Chapter 18: No One Ever Leaves a Star (1:34:35)

Summary: *Joe tells Norma he is leaving her; she shoots and kills him.*

This chapter is the climax of the film. After Betty leaves, Joe mounts the staircase in step with the staccato notes of Waxman's score, walking impassively past Norma and shutting the door to his room. In a revealing shot, Norma looks in the hall mirror, taking off her face patches and fluffing her hair, before striking a pose in preparation for the scene with Joe. The heavy baroque frame of the mirror embodies artifice.

The frantic incredulity on Norma's face when she realises that Joe really intends to leave her is filmed in close-up, emphasising her inability to face unpalatable truths. In desperation, she tries to appeal to her lover's greed, then threatens to shoot herself. Unmoved, Joe is again filmed from below. For the first time in their relationship, he is candid with Norma, telling her that she'd be killing herself to an empty house: 'The audience left twenty years ago.'

The story of Salome is woven through *Sunset Boulevard* and a parallel is set up between Norma and King Herod's lustful stepdaughter. Like Salome, Norma is proud and unforgiving. Just as Salome is spurned by John the Baptist and seeks her revenge by demanding his death, Norma kills Joe when he rejects her. The drama is reflected in the score. As Joe leaves the house, we hear a more foreboding version of the main theme, which becomes increasingly strident, until the fatal shots bring the music to a violent halt.

Q What does Norma see when she looks at herself in the mirror?

Q Look closely at the lighting and editing in this chapter. How do these elements contribute to the escalating sense of crisis?

Chapter 19: 'All right Mr. DeMille, I'm ready for my closeup.' (1:39:13)

Summary: *The house is surrounded by press and police; Joe's body is fished out of the pool; Norma has a complete breakdown.*

A dissolve connects Norma's fixated stare with the extraordinary 'fish's view' of Joe, floating face down in the pool. The voice-over signals a return to the opening murder scene; the narrative has come full circle. The pool, which Joe had always wanted, forms part of the unholy bargain he struck with Norma. Now the trappings of success have become painfully irrelevant, and Joe is only able to appreciate the irony of his situation from beyond the grave.

The film's black humour escalates in direct proportion to the seriousness of the situation. Nowhere is Joe's cynicism more in evidence than when his corpse is being photographed and fished out of the water. Commenting on the media circus gathered at the house, he notes, 'Here was an item everybody could have some fun with.'

Joe's body is taken away, and real-life society columnist Hedda Hopper picks up the narrative, dictating the story to her editor. Norma refuses to come downstairs, until she hears the magic word 'cameras'. Wilder uses a close-up to convey this key moment; Norma is about to get her wish and make a film again. The concluding image of the actress, lost in her mad celluloid fantasy, almost conveys the sense that she is being swallowed up by the cameras. Powerful chords signify the ending of the film as Norma's face dissolves into a white-out.

Q Do you feel any sympathy for Norma at this point? If so, how does Wilder elicit it?

CHARACTERS & RELATIONSHIPS

Norma Desmond (Gloria Swanson)

Key quotes

'Was her life really as empty as that?' (Joe, 0:25:29)

'Great stars have great pride.' (0:51:52)

'DeMille always said I was his greatest star.' (0:55:21)

Narcissistic, histrionic and self-deluded, Norma Desmond is a mass of neuroses and contradictions, a 'bundle of raw nerves'. Discovered as a teenager, she was one of the great luminaries of the early film industry but now, like Miss Havisham, lives in obscurity, with only her memories to sustain her. DeMille describes her as being a 'lovely little girl of seventeen with more courage and wit and heart than ever came together in one youngster', and clearly many at Paramount still remember her with great affection – although towards the end of her career Norma earned an unenviable reputation as a 'terror' to work with.

Norma is apparently a wealthy woman, yet she only retains one servant and her house exudes an air of neglect. She is deeply suspicious of strangers and when Joe first meets her, before he puts a name to the face, her first instinct is to have him thrown out. It seems that Norma does not *want* to be identified, preferring to live in anonymity rather than let the world know how far she has fallen. She does not want to be an object of curiosity or pity. Nor does she care to see herself through others' eyes.

Joe is perceptive enough to recognise early on that fear underpins Norma's reclusive lifestyle: 'The plain fact was that she was afraid of that world outside, afraid it would remind her that time had passed.' She has 'moments of melancholy' and has attempted suicide on more than one occasion. On the advice of Norma's physician, Max has gone into damage control: there are no locks on the doors, and no sleeping pills or razor blades are permitted in the house.

Underneath her imperious manner, Norma is desperately lonely. She has had three husbands (and, presumably, many lovers) but at fifty her life is so empty that she has adopted a chimpanzee as her companion. Until Joe's arrival, she spends most of her time indoors, often wearing sunglasses; the only light Norma has ever been comfortable with is the spotlight. Joe soon discovers that she deplores the current film industry from which, as a silent-movie star, she is now marginalised: 'We didn't need dialogue; we had faces.' Notwithstanding, she has written a screenplay, *Salome*, which she imagines will be the vehicle for her comeback.

Paradoxically, Norma's insecurity is only matched by her self-belief, and she is incapable of making a distinction between her celluloid self and reality. It is of the utmost importance to Norma that people should 'want' her; this craving for personal affirmation blinds her to the truth about her fans. Equating an audience's adulation with love leaves her bereft when it is no longer forthcoming. This vulnerability disarms DeMille when Norma visits Paramount, and he does not have the heart to reject her 'appalling' script out of hand. Similarly, Max understands Norma's fragility although, to an extent, he plays on it. By shielding her from the unpalatable truth that her fans stopped caring years ago, he simply compounds her delusions.

Norma's moods are mercurial – she can oscillate between charm and fury in an instant. Single-minded and egocentric, she is also an arch-manipulator. Having wielded power since she was a teenager, she is used to getting her own way and is ill-equipped to cope with denial or rejection. Threats, coercion and emotional blackmail all come naturally to her. Intuitively, she always plays to her audience. When Norma *does* get what she wants, her mood is sunny. When she encounters resistance, whether it is half-hearted – such as Joe's reluctance to stay at the palazzo – or decisive – as is the case when he walks out on New Year's Eve – she calibrates her response accordingly. However, she overplays her hand when her irrational jealousy prompts her to phone Betty, spearheading the final confrontation with Joe.

Norma's refusal to accept reality proves to be her downfall. While her reasons for purchasing a gun might be oblique, shooting her lover is a categorical rejection of the facts he presents to her, both in relation to her abortive screenplay and the demise of their relationship. She is appalled when Joe announces that he is leaving her: 'No one ever leaves a star.' Max does his ex-wife a great kindness in offering her an escape route from the brutal scrutiny of police and reporters. Taking refuge in madness, Norma is protected from the consequences of her actions; instead, imagining herself to be reliving the limelight, she believes she is making a picture for her adoring fans.

Key point

Norma is Hollywood's creation, epitomising its archetypal glamour and success as well as its moral failures. Like many stars who burn bright, Norma falls victim to, and is ultimately destroyed by, her narcissistic inability to relinquish her own celebrity.

Joe Gillis (William Holden)

Key quotes

'Just a movie writer with a couple of B pictures to his credit.' (0:02:25)

'Apparently I just didn't have what it takes.' (0:10:05)

'I don't qualify for the job, not anymore.' (1:36:20)

Joe Gillis is a talented but disillusioned scriptwriter who has come to Hollywood to make his fortune. A former reporter, he has written short stories and screenplays with modest success, but is now down on his luck and trying to stay one jump ahead of the finance company that wants to repossess his car. To that end, he lies about the car's whereabouts when the company reps are hounding him. Joe's ethical elasticity is born of necessity. Struggling financially, he cannot afford to be overly scrupulous; pride is no longer an option. Hence, he justifies the choices he has made as a hack writer. Hollywood is such a self-interested, dog-eat-dog environment that those who are not prepared to be opportunistic will be left behind. When fate throws Joe what appears to be a lifeline in the form of Norma Desmond, he takes it.

Initially, at least, Joe's manipulation of the situation is reasonable; Norma needs a writer to edit her script and he can, in good conscience, deliver. His subsequent exploitation of Norma's desire for companionship is more questionable. Incrementally, he allows himself to become more and more compromised. Norma's increasing fondness for her unexpected guest is clear and, disingenuously, Joe does little to discourage it. Allowing her to buy him expensive clothes is easier than arguing; Joe decides that the best approach is to humour her. He often takes refuge in irony to deflect moments of awkwardness or emotional intensity. As Norma's feelings for him become obvious, he tries to joke his way out of the situation: 'Come midnight, how about blindfolding the orchestra and smashing glasses over Max's head?'

Inevitably, though, Norma's declaration of love and her assumptions about their future together bring home to Joe the claustrophobic nature of their relationship. His first instinct is to escape: 'I had to be with people my own age.' Yet he returns to the palazzo without hesitation after Norma's suicide attempt. This critical decision alters the dynamic between the pair. Joe is no longer in control – if, indeed, he ever was. For all his miscalculations and weaknesses, he is, at heart, a decent man who does not want to inflict unnecessary hurt on a lonely woman. Because of this, he is susceptible to the emotional blackmail that is Norma's stock in trade and he allows himself to be manipulated by her apparent vulnerability. At the same time, Joe is complicit in his own downfall, taking the comfortable way out and rationalising the situation because it solves his financial problems: 'An older woman who's well-to-do. A younger man who's not doing too well.'

However, the arrangement becomes problematic when Joe wants his own life back – professionally and romantically. Good-looking and confident, he is used to ingratiating himself with women. When he first meets Betty, he automatically slips into flirtatious gear. Similarly, he uses his charm when he is trying to get back into her good books at the studio. While Joe recognises the inadvisability of pursuing a relationship with her – however innocent – he cannot resist the professional lure she dangles in front of him. For her part, Betty believes that Joe has a genuine, original talent; her faith in him, and her insistence that he can do better, encourages him to return to screenwriting.

Arguably, Joe shows the same determined myopia with Betty as he originally did with Norma, blocking out the growing evidence of her affection for him. When he does discover that she loves him, it seems to come as a surprise. Nevertheless, his feelings for Betty trigger his resolve to be a better man and shame him into breaking off the affair with Norma. He despises himself for succumbing to Norma's demands at the expense of his own ambition and independence. While he has always regarded returning to Dayton as an admission of failure, he is ultimately so full of self-loathing that it seems a fitting penance for the hurt he has inflicted. When he turns his back on Norma and the life she offers, Joe is also rejecting, more broadly, the values that underpin her world. Leaving the palazzo, he displays an undeniable, albeit short-lived, dignity. The final image of the murdered writer is described with Joe's trademark irony: 'Funny how gentle people get with you once you're dead.'

Key point

Joe pays dearly for his mistakes. In the end, like John the Baptist, he becomes a martyr, sacrificed to Norma's hubris.

Max von Mayerling (Erich von Stroheim)

Key quotes

'I pegged him as slightly cuckoo, too.' (Joe, 0:24:19)

'I made her a star. And I cannot let her be destroyed.' (1:22:01)

Loyal and dogged, Norma's first husband is an enigmatic figure, still in love with his ex-wife and utterly devoted to her care. Max was one of the three most promising directors of the silent era, but gave up his career to act as Norma's domestic retainer. In this capacity, he has watched a succession of husbands and lovers pass through her life. Max seems reconciled to his choice and accepts Joe's presence impassively. Knowing Norma as he does, he anticipates her interest in their new guest, making up the bed in the guest room before Joe has committed to staying. Max's only emotional release – and perhaps an expression of his true dislike of the arrangement – is to play the organ very loudly after Norma has dispatched him to fetch Joe's typewriter and clothes.

Max has made himself indispensable to Norma; if she needs anything, or anything goes wrong, her strident bray, 'Maaax ...' echoes through the house. Having morphed from husband into servant, Max's relationship with his employer is now a bizarre mixture of formality and intimacy. On the one hand, he always places a distance between himself and Norma by speaking to her, or about her, in the third person: 'Madame will ...' On the other, he does not hesitate to involve himself in matters that are not normally within the scope of an employee. For example, as they drive to Paramount, Max, observing Norma closely in the rear-view mirror, tells her that 'the shadow over the left eye is not quite balanced' – advice that Norma receives as a matter of course.

Fiercely protective of his former wife, Max is still, in many ways, trying to direct her life. He feeds Joe information on a need-to-know basis, evading questions he doesn't want to answer and encouraging Joe's sympathy for the actress. Similarly, he manipulates Joe's return to the mansion on New Year's Eve. Max also takes it upon himself to intercept Betty's phone calls when she tries to contact Joe. After the shooting, Max steps back into his directorial role to assist the police and get Norma out of the house.

However, in shielding Norma from the brutal fact that her career is well and truly over, Max simply exacerbates her illusions. As the sole author of the fan mail she receives, Max panders to Norma's belief that she is still wanted and admired. Like his erstwhile protégé, Max thinks in absolutes: 'Madame is the greatest star of them all.' In this sense, irrespective of whether he, too, is convinced that she can make a comeback, Max is almost as deluded as Norma herself.

Betty Schaefer (Nancy Olson)

Key quotes

'I just think that pictures should say a little something.' (0:06:40)

'What's wrong with being on the other side of the cameras? It's really more fun.' (1:19:31)

Betty is the antithesis of Norma: guileless, self-effacing, honest and brave. She comes from a 'picture family' and, as a child, the movie lot was her playground. Her parents and grandmother all worked at Paramount; in turn, Betty now works as a reader for the producer, Sheldrake. She is incisive and efficient – a two-page synopsis of *Bases Loaded* accompanies her brief oral report – and she has kept her optimism, despite her cynical boss and her own awareness of the industry's pitfalls.

Betty still believes passionately that films should be based on truth and explore something worthwhile. Joe disparagingly calls her 'one of the message kids'. Their first meeting is prickly as she is the reader who reviews Joe's latest script and advises Sheldrake against it. Betty is smart enough to recognise poor writing and candid enough to state her professional opinion frankly: 'I found it flat and trite.' She is very grounded and, just as she is realistic about her shortcomings as an actress, she knows her limitations as a writer, telling Joe, 'I'm just not good enough to do [the screenplay] all by myself.'

At the same time, Betty is ambitious; she knows what she wants and is hungry to learn. She sees Joe's story, 'Dark Windows', as an opportunity to make the transition from reader to screenwriter. After lengthy efforts to track Joe down, she pushes him to return to the project and is angry when he reneges on their (admittedly loose) arrangement: 'It's not your career, it's mine.'

As their script inches towards completion, Betty is faced with a stark choice: either be honest with Joe – a man she still does not know much about – or marry a decent man with whom she is no longer in love. When she finds out about Joe's relationship with Norma, Betty has the courage to forgive him, giving him the opportunity to put the past behind him: 'I never got those telephone calls and I've never been in this house.' The complete contrast between her and Norma is part of Betty's attraction for Joe; her transparent integrity throws Norma's duplicity into sharp relief. By his own admission, Joe is 'crazy' about her. However, convinced that he doesn't deserve her, he gives Betty up. In doing so, he seriously underestimates her, effectively robbing her of the opportunity to exercise her own choice.

Artie Green (Jack Webb)

Key quote

'You couldn't find a nicer guy.' (Joe, 1:11:02)

Artie is an assistant director, one of the many thousands who are trying to work their way up the Hollywood ladder. By general consensus, he is 'an awful nice guy', the type who would bend over backwards to help a friend, and Joe calls him a 'pal'. He is one of the few people in Hollywood that Joe trusts. Loyal and good-natured, Artie is prepared to lend Joe money without asking questions, even though he doesn't have much himself. With typical generosity, he hosts a large New Year's Eve party for dozens of his friends and colleagues. He even provides most of the booze, although his budget only extends to 'three drinks per extra'. When Joe turns up unannounced and asks if he can stay for a few days, Artie does not hesitate, offering the current 'vacancy on the couch'.

While Artie jokingly warns Joe off Betty, he trusts Betty implicitly. Working on location in Arizona, he spontaneously suggests that Betty join him so they can get married. Artie is 'as nice a guy that ever lived', and Joe knows that he falls short by comparison. In giving Betty up, Joe assumes that she will return to her fiancé: 'Well, you and Artie can be admirable.' This is perhaps another hopeful rationalisation on Joe's part, but it would be in keeping with Artie's character to forgive the woman he loves and encourage her to put the past behind her.

Sheldrake (Fred Clark)

Key quote

'He was a smart producer, with a set of ulcers to prove it.' (Joe, 0:05:07)

According to Joe, the cigar-chewing Sheldrake is a 'big shot' at Paramount Pictures. Hard-nosed, cynical and brash, he is described as smart, but he has had his failures. He ruefully admits that he passed up the script of *Gone with the Wind* – winner of ten Academy Awards and the highest-grossing film ever made in Hollywood – on the mistaken assumption that no one would want to see a Civil War picture. Sheldrake relies on his staff to sift through the scripts that land on his desk, but he can't be bothered remembering their names, introducing Betty as 'Miss Kramer'.

While Sheldrake has supported Joe in the past and is prepared to hear him out – 'All right Gillis. You've got five minutes' – he is risk-averse and does not believe in throwing away good money. He declines to lend Joe money, giving him a droll, longwinded explanation of the financial difficulties in which this would place him. The false congeniality with which the producer sees Joe off, arm around his shoulders, gives the impression that he is doing Joe a favour.

Cecil B. DeMille (as himself)

Key quote

'There were three young directors who showed promise in those days: DW Griffith, Cecil B. DeMille and Max von Mayerling.' (Max, 1:22:13)

We hear a great deal about DeMille before we meet him. If a man's success can be measured by the number of underlings required to convey a message to him, then Cecil B. DeMille is a very important man indeed. News of Norma's arrival at Paramount is passed along a hierarchical line of increasingly important employees until it reaches DeMille himself. Famous and highly regarded, he has been working in the industry since its inception and has climbed to the pinnacle of his profession. Norma is particular about who should direct her brainchild; DeMille – with whom she has worked in the past – is the only director she considers.

DeMille has a paternalistic relationship with Norma. Despite her own age and status, she still calls him 'Mr DeMille', and when he looks at her he sees the feisty adolescent who conquered Paramount thirty years earlier. DeMille is sympathetic to the former star's position. It would be easy to give Norma 'the brush', as his assistant suggests, but such unkindness does not sit easily with him. When she makes her unexpected visit to the studio, the director stops the shoot and welcomes her with open arms. He even sits her in his own chair as they talk. DeMille is dignified, measured and tactful, telling the actress gently, 'You know Norma, pictures have changed quite a bit'. While he does not commit to *Salome* – suggesting that the decision would not rest with him alone – he does what he can to spare her feelings, including instructing Gordon Cole to shelve the idea of using the Isotta Fraschini as a movie prop.

THEMES, IDEAS & VALUES

Reality and illusion

Key quotes

'… still waving proudly to a parade which had long since passed her by.' (Joe, 0:39:25)

'There's nothing tragic about being fifty. Not unless you try to be twenty-five.' (Joe, 1:37:50)

Sunset Boulevard explores the interplay between illusion and reality in a number of ways. At the most basic level, the film acknowledges the role cinema plays in creating and fostering illusion. Watching a film is an immersive experience that allows an audience to escape from reality for a short time. This world of illusion is richer, and certainly more entertaining, than the messy problems of most people's real lives. As the stories on the screen unfold, audiences can indulge in their own private fantasies; they become invested in the characters and lose themselves in the moment. Norma understands this symbiotic relationship better than most, paying tribute to 'those wonderful people out there in the dark' who are on the journey with her.

In order to highlight the sometimes tenuous demarcation between illusion and reality, Wilder deliberately blurs the lines, playing with the audience's perception of what is real and what is not. For example, several real-life celebrities – director Cecil B. DeMille, gossip columnist Hedda Hopper, and silent screen star Buster Keaton – play themselves. The names of Hollywood identities – including actor Alan Ladd, actress Greta Garbo and producer Darryl Zanuck – are sprinkled throughout the film.

Furthermore, the experiences of key characters often overlap with those of the actors themselves. Like Norma Desmond, Gloria Swanson was a star of the silent movie era, and photos of her in her heyday are displayed in Norma's salon. Erich von Stroheim and DeMille both directed Swanson in a number of films and DeMille called her 'Young fella', which is how he greets Norma when she visits Paramount. This appropriation of the real world even extends to the locations. The actual Paramount Studios buildings were used for relevant scenes in *Sunset Boulevard*, including the iconic Bronson gate, the offices and the sets. Schwab's Pharmacy on Sunset Boulevard was a haunt of Hollywood insiders and those aspiring to get into the industry.

Hollywood is the quintessential dream factory, a magnet attracting a huge array of talented, and not-so-talented, individuals who want to be part of the Hollywood movie industry success story. However, the film shows that not all dreams come true, and the reality is often very different. Joe, for example, has come to Los Angeles from Dayton, Ohio, where he worked as a reporter on the local paper. While he has a couple of B-grade pictures to his credit, when we first meet him he is prostituting his talent, desperately pitching rewrites to Paramount. He owes money and, in his own words, his prospects add up to 'exactly zero'.

Joe soon learns that Norma is still 'sleepwalking along the giddy heights of a lost career'. Her inability to let go of the past has enmeshed her in a web of delusion. Norma's refusal to see herself as anything other than a great star is reinforced by her reclusive lifestyle. She has as little to do with the real world as possible; the only people she socialises with are, similarly, relics of the silent movie era. The fiction of Norma's ongoing fame is bolstered by Max, who colludes with his ex-wife by feeding her lies and writing her fan mail. The vehicle for Norma's 'return' will be the script she has written – a script she is convinced DeMille will accept with alacrity. Moreover, there is no doubt in the actress' mind that she will be the only choice to play the vengeful adolescent, Salome. Surrounded by her own images, frozen in time, Norma's illusionary sense of self remains unchallenged.

Norma's meeting with Joe coincides with her planned comeback. Their subsequent 'romance' is another fantasy on her part, concocted out of loneliness and her inability to entertain the idea that Joe might not reciprocate her infatuation. On New Year's Eve, she confesses her feelings to Joe, detailing elaborate plans that reveal the sizeable emotional investment she has already made in their relationship. For his part, Joe knows that the relationship is unsustainable; for him, it is a hiatus from reality that provides a temporary respite from the Hollywood treadmill that has, to date, consumed all of his energy and ambition.

Norma is not the only star who implicitly believes her own publicity, but she is an extreme example. She has built her life on an illusionary sense of self and she cannot, or will not, hear the truth: 'I am a star … the greatest star of them all.' Joe's early instinct proves to be correct: 'You don't yell at a sleepwalker. He may fall and break his neck.' When he tries to shatter Norma's delusions, she snaps. By the end of the film, when she imagines herself back at Paramount making a film for her devoted fans, she is completely disconnected from reality.

Hollywood

Key quotes

'Hollywood for us ain't been so good.
Got no swimming pool. Very few clothes.
All we earn are buttons and bows.' (Artie's party, 0:45:21)

'You know, some crazy things happen in this business, Norma.' (DeMille, 1:07:51)

Hollywood is a modern frontier and, like the gold rush pioneers of California's past, the individuals who flock to the city are driven by a hunger and determination to prosper. When Joe is brought face to face with Betty's resolve to be a writer, he recognises his younger self: 'She was so like all us writers when we first hit Hollywood. Itching with ambition, panting to get your names up there.'

Hollywood is full of narcissistic personalities, inflated expectations and aggressive rivalries. It is an intensely competitive environment in which opportunism flourishes. Sheldrake's stomach ulcers are testimony to the pressure felt by producers and others working in the industry. Further, the relentless pursuit of money and fame challenges an individual's personal and professional integrity. Joe's cynical advice to Norma – 'Never let another writer read your material; he may steal it' – is presumably based on experience.

In general, writers do not have an easy time of it in Hollywood. Wilder employs the familiar trope of writers as the most undervalued component in the creative pecking order, regarded as interchangeable and easily replaced. Indeed, they often have to suffer the indignity of extensive rewrites that can render their original work virtually unrecognisable. Joe ruefully tells Norma that, by the time it reached the screen, his last script – originally about Okies in the dust bowl (agricultural workers affected by drought in the prairies) – ended up being set on a torpedo boat. Like most writers, Joe accepts these disappointments phlegmatically, because he has to. After a long apprenticeship in Hollywood, he is under no illusions as to what kind of writing will pay the rent: 'Who wants true? Who wants moving?' Conversely, 'psychopaths sell like hot cakes'.

This ongoing tension between art and profit is one of many contradictions that underpin the world of Hollywood. Sheldrake's farcical suggestion to turn Joe's baseball script into a vehicle for Betty Hutton (star of *Annie Get Your Gun*) is indicative of the contortions producers go through to make square pegs fit into round holes. Even Joe thinks he is joking. To achieve a balance between artistic credibility and commercial viability is a constant challenge, partly due to the prescribed expectations of the studios – everything is written to a recipe. Betty complains, 'So you take plot 27, make it glossy, make it slick.' At Artie's party, she and Joe lampoon some of the romantic stereotypes when they adopt the clichéd dialogue regularly depicted on the screen.

However, although Hollywood scripts might conform to a formula, movie-making is not an exact science – a paradox highlighted by Sheldrake's mistake in passing up *Gone with the Wind*. Joe sums up the mercurial nature of the business when he says, 'I talked to a couple of yes-men at Metro. To me, they said no.' There is no room for sentiment.

A director like DeMille has to make hard-headed decisions based on commercial viability. Nor are these decisions unilateral; they are subject to scrutiny. Despite his obvious affection for Norma, DeMille cannot endorse a bad script simply out of old loyalties.

The film obliquely references the competition between movies and the theatre; specifically Hollywood and Broadway (New York). The theatre world is viewed by some – most particularly those who work in it – as culturally and artistically superior, while the film industry exemplifies brash commercialism. Hence, when Sheldrake accuses Betty and Joe of sounding 'like a bunch of New York critics', he is implying that they are on a very different page to film producers such as himself. Even so, 'glossy' and 'slick' are considered dirty words in Hollywood. Those in the industry don't like being reminded of the fact that making money is their bottom line.

Running in tandem with Wilder's cynical understanding of what makes Hollywood tick is a genuine affection for the people who make movies. Herein lies another paradox – the many opposing interests and competing egos are at odds with the essentially collaborative nature of filmmaking. The controlled chaos of the *Samson and Delilah* set is a reminder of the sheer number of people required to produce a film, as well as an acknowledgement of the exceptional creativity that underpins the task.

Betty herself is a third-generation child of Hollywood; her father was the head electrician at Paramount, her mother still works in wardrobe, and her grandmother did stunt work for Pearl White (a silent-movie star). Initially Betty went through the usual hoops, trying to become an actress, until she realised that her talent and inclination lay behind the cameras. And in spite of her own awareness of Hollywood's more ruthless underbelly, she is not immune to its magic. Strolling through the studio's 'drowsing' lot at night, she tells Joe that it is her favourite street in the world. In spite, or perhaps because of the fact that it is 'all cardboard, all hollow, all phoney, all done with mirrors', we are invited to share her enthusiasm.

Love

Key quotes

'What you're trying to say is you don't want me to love you.' (Norma, 0:43:29)

'Hey Joe, I said you could have my couch. I didn't say you could have my girl.' (Artie, 0:47:48)

In *Sunset Boulevard,* love and those who profess to feel it are mercilessly scrutinised. Throughout the text, love that is destructive and ego-driven is juxtaposed with genuinely unselfish love. Sometimes the lines are blurred. Love can be bound up with betrayal, and good people can deliberately hurt those to whom they are closest.

Norma's most important, and enduring, love affair is with herself. The feeling of being desired fuels her ego, offering her the attention she craves – even if the relationship is based on little more than opportunism and mutual convenience. Norma is attracted to Joe simply on the basis of his availability. When he appears at the palazzo, she is hostile, but this quickly morphs into interest when she discovers he is a writer. Her learning that he is single seals his fate. Norma wants to be in love – 'I like Sagittarians, you can trust them' – and it doesn't really matter with whom. Their subsequent relationship is essentially transactional. Joe offers Norma companionship – having an attractive younger man as her escort bolsters her self-image – and she keeps Joe in a manner to which he becomes easily accustomed. As Joe cynically describes it: 'I've got a good deal here. A long-term contract with no options.'

Norma equates love with possession. Wilder continually draws attention to her hands, claw-like and predatory, as a symbol of her possessiveness. She attempts to smooth out Joe's rough edges; his sophisticated wardrobe is just the start of a campaign to improve his image. Norma teaches her reluctant boyfriend how to play bridge and dance the tango, and educates him about which wines and food go together. She even instructs him not to chew gum.

However, the power balance between Joe and Norma begins to shift when he finds himself falling in love with Betty Schaefer. The two are immediately attracted to each other, which they hide behind parody. This is risky territory for them both, after all. Betty is already in a relationship with Artie, who also happens to be a good friend of Joe's. Up until the point where Joe and Betty acknowledge their love, Joe resolutely maintains a teasing tone, designed to undercut the chemistry between them. Nevertheless, despite his determination not to become involved, Joe is drawn to Betty's passion and candour. Their script, 'Untitled Love Story', is the vehicle that brings them together, and the idea of a couple sharing common professional ground is mirrored in the script itself.

Inevitably, when faced with Betty's emotional honesty, Joe is reminded of the unsavoury aspects of his own lifestyle. In the end, he loves Betty – and hates himself – too much to seriously consider making a life with her. Comparing himself with the uncomplicated devotion and security that Artie offers, Joe feels so completely unworthy that he is left with no choice but to reject Betty. Although she is badly hurt in the process, Joe is willing to put his own interests aside for the sake of the one he loves, which is exactly what Norma refuses to do. When Joe announces that he is finally leaving her, Norma is desperate enough to offer him money – an offer that reflects badly on them both. She also brandishes her gun. This time, though, Joe calls Norma's bluff. He has had enough of her emotional blackmail and is no longer prepared to rationalise her threats of suicide as a reason to stay.

In *Sunset Boulevard*, the explicit correlation between love and sacrifice is also played out in Max's relationship with Norma. After she left him, Max found life so 'unendurable' that he was prepared to abandon a promising, high-profile career and become her servant, 'humiliating as it may seem'. That this was motivated by love is not in doubt. At the same time, Max's love is shown to be inextricably entwined with ego. Much of his devotion is predicated on pride as well as genuine adoration. Norma Desmond was his creation – 'I discovered her when she was sixteen' – and he refuses to 'let her be destroyed', partially because his own self-worth is also invested in her celebrity.

Key point

In the text, love is depicted as a dangerous emotion. However, while Joe's relationship with Norma is demeaning, compromising both his self-respect and his autonomy, his love for Betty is redemptive, encouraging him to ultimately step away from his dependence on Norma.

Fame

Key quotes

'I'm not just selling the script, I'm selling me.' (Norma, 0:55:18)

'And teach your friend some manners. Tell him without me, he wouldn't have any job, because without me, there wouldn't be any Paramount Studio.' (Norma, 1:02:55)

In Hollywood, success and fame are two sides of the same coin. During the early years of the film industry, Norma's fame was unprecedented and she made a fortune out of her celebrity. Max tells Joe that 'she was the greatest of them all', receiving 17 000 fan letters a week. Infamously, a smitten Indian maharajah strangled himself with one of her discarded stockings.

Like other stars of the silent era, Norma led a life of excess. Her palazzo was ostentatious, 'the kind crazy movie people built in the crazy twenties', with a pool, tennis court and the unheard-of luxury of a home cinema. Her car, the handmade, imported Isotta Fraschini, had leopard-skin upholstery and a gold-plated telephone. Making '$18 000 a week and no taxes', actors made famous by the silver screen had wealth beyond most people's dreams and, in a secular society, were deified. Audiences neither wanted nor expected their idols to be ordinary, which virtually gave stars permission to behave outrageously, without the constraints that applied to lesser mortals. When Norma visits Paramount, she tells DeMille, 'The last time I saw you was someplace very gay … I was dancing on a table.'

However, Hollywood has a destructive edge. Fame is ephemeral and the text argues strongly that, even if individuals achieve the success they crave, there is always a cost. Norma is one of many to fall victim to the cult of celebrity. 'Norma Desmond' was, of course, a carefully crafted construct, the product of studio expectations and the Paramount publicity machine. Norma's life has been lived in the public gaze since she was a teenager, and her sense of self has been shaped by 'a dozen press agents working overtime' and the adulation of the public. DeMille is sensitive to the damage done to impressionable young psyches by this process, suggesting that Norma's reputation as a 'terror' to work with was the demonstrable result. A lifetime of being fawned over, with her every whim indulged, means that she is incapable of making any distinction between her public persona and her private self.

Norma was not the only actress who started in her teens. The industry makes huge demands; young stars are worked hard, aspiring candidates even harder. The many references to faces in the text highlight the importance of optics in the movie business. If faces are not perfect, then they must be made so. This is why ingenues such as Betty subject themselves to nose jobs, extensive dental work and other surgical enhancements at the behest of the studios. Norma's face has literally been her fortune, and all her working life she has been taught to regard it as a precious commodity. In this sense, her narcissism is as predictable as it is uncompromising. Twenty years after her career has finished, she is convinced of the value of her face: 'I can say anything I want with my eyes.'

Importantly, Norma is still defining success on the screen by the criteria of the past. Her characterisation of talent only extends as far as the visual; she does not seem to understand that a beautiful face in itself is no longer enough. If it were, the attrition rate for actors trying to make the transition to talkies would not have been so high. Norma is dismissive of the current crop of faces on offer – only Garbo measures up – and the truism that cinema is still – always – full of attractive faces seems lost on her. Planning her comeback, she feels intense pressure to look her best and, to that end, employs an army of beauticians to work on her physical appearance.

Joe's fate underscores the dubious line between fame and notoriety. Like so many others, he has come to Hollywood to make a success of his writing career, an objective aborted by his relationship with the actress. While he dreads returning to Dayton with his tail between his legs, by the time he has decided to leave Norma, he understands that it is not the worst outcome. Success as a screenwriter no longer seems the priority, and he is more interested in salvaging his self-respect. Posthumously, though, Joe achieves the prominence he desired. The morning after his death, press and police gather at the palazzo. His lifeless body is photographed and his affair with Norma will be dissected and laid out for public consumption. From now on, he will be the subject of salacious headlines and fodder for gossip columnists, and his name will be inextricably associated with that of Norma Desmond. Thus, Joe pays the highest price for Norma's vanity and the culture that has spawned it.

Key point

Norma's lament that 'they took the idols and smashed them' overlooks the real point. Fame itself is a poisoned chalice, containing a toxic mechanism that destroys careers and reputations, not to mention psyches. In Norma's case, her desperation to recapture the limelight is the very thing that breaks her.

Gender roles

Key quotes

'Well, seems like Zanuck has got himself a baseball picture.' (Sheldrake, 0:07:13)

'My father was head electrician here 'til he died. Mother still works in wardrobe.' (Betty, 1:18:42)

At face value, Hollywood is an atypical milieu, unique due to its glamour and creativity. At the same time, it is also a microcosm that mirrors the conservative values of the wider community. In particular, the roles assumed by the men in the text signal the dominant patriarchal ethos of postwar American society. It is men who hold positions of authority and influence: producers, directors, screenwriters and agents are male. Film actresses – even the most successful – are strictly contracted to the studio system that is controlled and headed by men, such as Darryl Zanuck at 20th Century-Fox.

The relationship between Sheldrake and the women who work for him demonstrates this power dynamic. The mise en scène in Sheldrake's large, spacious office reveals all the trappings of success. He has a pleasant view from his window and a couch to lie on. An Oscar is mounted in pride of place and there are other trophies on various shelves. Framed awards and testimonials cover the walls, as well as photos of the stars the producer has worked with. By contrast, Betty's office is a 'cubby-hole' that had previously been a dressing room. Sheldrake takes his female staff for granted; as far as he is concerned, they are interchangeable and forgettable. For instance, he confuses Betty with a Miss Kramer. Sheldrake takes even less notice of his secretary, who comes in for the sole purpose of handing him his tablets even though the pill bottle is sitting right in front of him.

The gender divide in Hollywood is not only evident in its power structures. The contrasting types of work that men and women do also reflect a traditional gender bias, underlining the established dichotomy between an active masculine role and a more passive feminine role. At Paramount Studios, women are more likely to be confined to office work or wardrobe, while a wider range of jobs is available to men. From the officials at the gate to the cinematographers and lighting technicians on the set, men are notably more visible. DeMille's fiefdom, Studio 18, in particular, is male-dominated territory.

On the other hand, relationships in the text do not necessarily conform to type. Hedda Hopper's appearance at the end of the film is an interesting example. Here she is the only woman, surrounded by a crush of men, insisting that her deadline is more important than the police doing their job. In the Hollywood hierarchy, the real-life Hopper's position was a singular one. As the town's foremost gossip columnist, she wielded considerable influence, disseminating selective information and damaging rumour in equal measure, which resulted in her being disliked, even feared, by the Hollywood fraternity.

By virtue of her wealth and status, Norma holds the upper hand in the relationship with Joe, who, in turn, has made himself utterly reliant on the actress' goodwill. Norma controls the purse strings, providing the roof over Joe's head, the clothes on his back and the food he eats. Even his car has been ignominiously towed away, increasing his dependence on her. When Joe starts working on the screenplay with Betty, he reclaims a small measure of independence, but this requires going behind Norma's back and misfires badly. Further, as Joe points out, there are no guarantees that this attempt to extricate himself from dependence on Norma will succeed: the script 'may sell and very possibly will not'.

Similarly, the dynamic between Norma and Max subverts the prevailing stereotype. Max's role is a submissive one, requiring him to acquiesce passively to Norma's demands, however outrageous or distasteful they may be. Norma treats Max with a casual lack of respect, born out of long familiarity. Although Max brings a stoic dignity to his role, being forced to watch as his ex-wife cavorts with her young lover is, by its nature, demeaning. It is only after Joe's murder that Max regains his authority. As director, he again takes control of the narrative.

Sunset Boulevard also addresses the issue of ageing for women. In Hollywood, it is youth and beauty that have currency. This has negative implications for women in particular, whose credibility in leading parts is seen to be limited by age. In 1950s Hollywood – and beyond – there was a clear double standard, skewed firmly in favour of men. Male stars were still playing romantic leads well into their sixties, whereas actresses of forty often struggled to secure desirable roles. Notwithstanding the fact that Norma has not successfully transitioned to talkies, the harsh reality is that by Hollywood standards, at the age of fifty she has passed her use-by date.

DIFFERENT INTERPRETATIONS

Different interpretations arise from different responses to a text. Over time, a text will evoke a wide range of responses from its readers, who may come from various social or cultural groups and live in very different places and historical periods. Responses by critics and reviewers can be published in newspapers, journals and books, both online and in print. They can also be expressed in discussions among readers in the media, classrooms, book groups and so on.

While there is no single correct reading or interpretation of a text, it is important to understand that an interpretation is more than a personal opinion – it is the justification of a point of view on a text. To present an interpretation of a text based on your point of view, you must use a logical argument and support it with relevant evidence from the text.

Critical viewpoints

Consistently cited as one of the top one hundred films ever made, *Sunset Boulevard* has continued to intrigue audiences and commentators in the decades since its first release. When *Sunset Boulevard* premiered in 1950, its critical reception was very favourable – in spite of the film's subject matter, which inevitably raised a few eyebrows. Thomas M Pryor, writing in *The New York Times*, called *Sunset Boulevard* 'a great motion picture', noting that Brackett and Wilder 'have kept an essentially tawdry romance from becoming distasteful and embarrassing'. Pryor did, however, express reservations about the film's ending, arguing that the narration by the dead Joe Gillis was 'a device completely unworthy of Brackett and Wilder' (Pryor 1950). *The Hollywood Reporter* had no such reservations, stating in another contemporary review that 'this completely original work' is 'marvellously satisfying, dramatically perfect, and technically brilliant' (THR staff 1950).

Inevitably, critics have focused on different aspects of the film. In particular though, its representation of Hollywood has generated considerable discussion. In his online review, Brian Eggert cites *Sunset Boulevard* as 'an inspired depiction of how Hollywood is a series of extravagant delusions, and a tale that demystifies the glamour and allure of fame' (Eggert 2016). Sam Staggs, in his book *Close-Up on Sunset Boulevard: Billy Wilder, Norma Desmond, and the Dark Hollywood Dream*, calls it a 'mordant elegy to the silent picture era' (Staggs 2002). Conversely, Pamela Hutchinson in *The Guardian* asserts that the 'true horror' of *Sunset Boulevard* is the way in which it explores the demise of the studio system: 'Desmond's pride mocks the fall of Hollywood, just as it was teetering, rocked by the anti-trust laws, the coming of TV and the communist witch-hunts' (Hutchinson 2016). Writing for *Variety*, William Brogdon observes that Wilder has used 'an iconoclastic approach that will help shatter the public's illusions and which does much to perpetuate filmland myths and idiosyncrasies' (Brogdon, 1950).

Roger Ebert argues that *Sunset Boulevard* remains 'the best drama ever made about the movies because it sees through the illusions'. But he also views it as a love story, suggesting that Max's devotion to the deluded Norma gives the film 'its emotional resonance', grounding it in reality despite its 'gothic flamboyance' (Ebert 1999). In an interesting piece for *The Guardian*, Tom Joudrey compares *Sunset Boulevard*'s indictment of celebrity with the twenty-first century's celebration of visibility: '*Sunset Boulevard* forces us to contemplate the cost of needing to be seen – namely, the unquenchable thirst for external validation that festers beneath a culture of exhibitionism'. For Joudrey, the film's relevance – and prescience – lies in the way it explores 'the surrender of selfhood that comes from living as a spectacle, in all its unforgiving, ruthless glory' (Joudrey 2020).

Two interpretations of *Sunset Boulevard*

Interpretation 1: *Sunset Boulevard* shows that the milieu of Hollywood makes it difficult to have close relationships.

In *Sunset Boulevard,* Hollywood is depicted as a climate that is far from conducive to establishing and maintaining close relationships. The intense competition to succeed and the endemic lack of trust breeds a self-serving mentality: everyone has to put their own interests first in this dog-eat-dog world, at both the professional and personal level.

Nobody in Hollywood does anything for nothing. Joe's longstanding associations with his agent and with Sheldrake have deteriorated in direct proportion to the reversal in his fortunes. Joe tells us that Sheldrake has 'always liked' him, but this does not extend to accepting an indifferent script or lending money. Joe cannot even solicit hack work out of the producer, who tells him 'there's nothing, honest'.

Joe's opinion of his agent is low – 'the big faker' – for good reason. When Joe finally does locate him on the golf course, it is clear that the agent has little interest in (or optimism about) finding work for his client. The suggestion that Joe will write better on an empty stomach simply adds insult to injury, as does the patently insincere counterclaim, 'I'm your friend'. Predictably, this exchange ends in acrimony, with Joe being told, 'Sweetheart, maybe what you need is another agent.' By his own admission, Joe is 'nobody important', so of course men like the agent are prepared to ditch him if and when necessary; there is no room in their industry for anything that does not sell.

The exploitation that thrives in the movie business bleeds into personal relationships. Ambition is ubiquitous, and everyone has an eye for the main chance. Even a character like Betty is not immune. She knows Joe by reputation – 'I'd always heard that you had some talent' – and homes in on the opportunity to work with him.

Furthermore, the text shows that most relationships in Hollywood are vulnerable. Romantic relationships often fall by the wayside. The temptations that arise from working long hours in close proximity to attractive colleagues means there are too few boundaries between work and play. Betty and Artie present as a happy couple engaged to be married, but this does not prevent Betty from falling in love with Joe. Similarly, Max loses Norma to husband Number Two, who in turn is replaced by husband Number Three. Friendships also suffer. Joe clearly thinks highly of Artie, but only gets in touch with him when he wants something.

Hollywood is a milieu in which egos flourish. Most individuals are too focused on themselves and their own needs to allow for true intimacy with others. Joe tells Norma, 'You're the only person in this stinking town that has been good to me.' While this is, in itself, an indictment of Hollywood, it is also a convenient rationalisation designed to make Joe feel better about his decision to stay with Norma. Yes, she has given him a job, but there are significant strings attached – notably, her insistence that he stay at her house. She does not pay Joe for his work; instead, she cherrypicks the ways in which she chooses to help him, to serve her own purpose. Gestures that appear to be generous, such as paying his overdue rent, only make Joe more beholden to her. Conversely, Norma will not save his car from repossession because she wants to be able to control and monitor his movements.

The exploitative nature of this relationship works both ways. After all, Joe also has an agenda; he is the one who 'dropped the hook and [Norma] snapped at it'. When Joe asks what gives Norma the right to make assumptions about their future together, he has lost the moral high ground and is forced to back down. By this stage, she has been keeping him for months and bought him an expensive wardrobe. The fiction that Joe is an independent contractor has long gone.

Los Angeles is a city of sprawling suburbs and freeways whose very layout does not encourage a sense of community. Joe argues that losing his car here would be akin to 'having [his] legs cut off'. The Boulevard itself is long and winding, with huge mansions that are set well back from the road and far apart from their neighbours. In this setting, Norma's reclusive lifestyle is easy to maintain. The Isotta Fraschini is on blocks when Joe first arrives at the palazzo, suggesting that the former star rarely ventures into the outside world. Her only social contact is when she and old colleagues meet for the strangely awkward bridge games. Despite the group's shared history, there is no warmth or conversation between them. Collectively, Joe dubs them 'the waxworks' because they face each other in unsmiling unison, unresponsive to anything except the game. Buster Keaton's one line is 'Pass'.

Sunset Boulevard presents relationships in Hollywood as shallow at best and exploitative at worst. 'Tinsel town' prioritises self-interest and money at the expense of loyalty and real connection.

Interpretation 2: *Sunset Boulevard* illustrates that Hollywood's film industry creates a genuine, distinctive bond between people.

Sunset Boulevard suggests that the Hollywood community is a close-knit one. In spite of, or perhaps because of, the intrinsic pressures placed upon them, there is a particular connection between people who work in the film industry.

Schwab's Pharmacy is a symbol of this fraternity. The drugstore is 'kind of a combination office, Kaffeeklatsch ['coffee chatter'] and waiting room' for actors and writers. In or out of work, Schwab's is their 'headquarters', the place where they meet and network, providing mutual solidarity in the face of (sometimes) flagging hopes. Joe may have fallen on hard times, but he is certainly not alone.

New Year's Eve demonstrates the fellowship that comes from shared experience in a tough industry. Artie's small apartment is crammed with his friends and colleagues. All have dreams in common. Joe describes them as 'writers without a job, composers without a publisher, actresses so young they still believed the guys in the casting office'. This is his tribe, and as soon as he arrives at the party he relaxes into its boozy, flirtatious atmosphere. The image of the group gathered around the piano, singing about the fickle returns for those trying to make it in the movie business ('all we earn are buttons and bows'), encapsulates their camaraderie.

The text shows that small unsolicited acts of kindness occur, even in a town as cynical as Hollywood. Joe's neighbour, Rudy, is sympathetic to his predicament and turns a blind eye when Joe hides his car behind the shoeshine parlour: 'Rudy never asked any questions about your finances; he'd just look at your heels and he'd know the score.' Rudy's wave in response to the toot of Joe's car horn indicates his solidarity. Artie himself is a loyal friend, the first person Joe thinks of when he is in trouble. Artie does not probe when Joe requests his help, simply lending him money and offering accommodation. Artie's comment regarding the current 'vacancy on the couch' suggests that Joe is not the only one to benefit from his generosity. Equally, Betty does not have to go out of her way to help Joe by resurrecting 'Dark Windows' and pitching the idea to Sheldrake. But she recognises Joe's talent and empathises with his situation.

Hollywood's real heart is the movie set, and it is here that a sense of true community is most in evidence. When Norma visits Paramount, it is a homecoming, a return to the family that adopted her when she was a teenager. Norma has not been on a set in twenty years – in fact, she last saw DeMille in 1927 – but those with whom she worked have long memories. As far as security guard Jonesy is concerned 'Miss Desmond' is still entitled to unfettered access to DeMille's inner sanctum of Stage 18. When Hog-eye turns the spotlight on the actress, it is a tribute to her enduring star presence. The genuine warmth and respect that the extras show Norma is touching; they mill around her, vying for her attention, while she accepts their good wishes like a queen.

DeMille's gallantry to Norma when she arrives at the studio is notable. Although he is in the middle of a shoot and her visit is unscheduled, the director refuses to give Norma 'the brush' as suggested by his assistant. Instead, he is tactful and affectionate, making her feel as welcome as possible. DeMille remembers his former protégé fondly as a lovely, spirited adolescent who took the movie world by storm. In order to spare Norma's feelings, he humours her regarding the dreadful script and stops Gordon Cole's attempts to hire her car.

Finally, the text implies, by omission, that Hollywood is such an insular and singular environment that there is little opportunity to form close relationships beyond its orbit. Betty's parents both worked behind the camera; Betty and Artie met through work; actresses, like Norma, marry their directors or other actors. While not all of these relationships last the distance, many do thrive. Long-term friendships are also forged by working together. By choice, Norma leads a quiet life, yet she does maintain regular contact with a small group of old friends who enjoy playing bridge together and, like her, are actors from the silent-movie days.

Sunset Boulevard certainly acknowledges the challenges and demands of working in Hollywood, and the impact these tensions can have on relationships. Even so, the environment's surface glamour and highly competitive nature do not preclude genuine bonds from developing and enduring.

QUESTIONS & ANSWERS

Essay writing – an overview

An essay on a literary work is a formal and serious piece of writing that presents your point of view on the text, usually in response to a given topic. Your 'point of view' in an essay is your interpretation of the meaning of the text's language, structure, characters, situations and events, supported by detailed analysis of textual evidence.

Analyse – don't summarise

In your essays it is important to avoid simply summarising what happens in a text.

- A **summary** is a description or paraphrase (retelling in different words) of the characters and events. For example: 'Macbeth has a horrifying vision of a dagger dripping with blood before he goes to murder King Duncan.'
- An **analysis** is an explanation of the real meaning or significance that lies 'beneath' the text's words (and images, for a film). For example: 'Macbeth's vision of a bloody dagger shows how deeply uneasy he is about the violent act he is contemplating, and conveys his sense that supernatural forces are impelling him to act.'

A limited amount of summary is sometimes necessary to let your reader know which part of the text you wish to discuss. However, always keep this to a minimum and follow it immediately with your analysis of what this part of the text is really telling us.

Plan your essay

Carefully plan your essay so that you have a clear idea of what you are going to say. The plan ensures that your ideas flow logically, that your argument remains consistent and that you stay on the topic. An essay plan should be a list of **brief dot points** covering no more than half a page.

- Include your central argument or main contention – a concise statement of your overall response to the topic.
- Write three or four dot points for each paragraph, indicating the main idea and evidence/examples from the text. Note that in your essay you will need to *expand* on these points and analyse the evidence.

Structure your essay

An essay is a complete, self-contained piece of writing. It has a clear beginning (the introduction), middle (several body paragraphs) and end (the last paragraph or conclusion). It must also have a central argument that runs throughout, linking each paragraph to form a coherent whole. See examples of introductions and conclusions in the 'Analysing a sample topic' and 'Sample answer' sections.

The introduction establishes your overall response to the topic. It includes your main contention and outlines the main evidence you will refer to in the course of the essay. Write your introduction *after* you have done a plan and *before* you write the rest of the essay.

The body paragraphs argue your case – they present evidence from the text and explain how this evidence supports your argument. Each body paragraph needs:

- a strong topic **sentence** (usually the first sentence) that states the main point being made in the paragraph
- **evidence** from the text, including some brief quotations
- **analysis** of the textual evidence, with **explanation** of its significance and how it supports your argument
- **links back to the topic** in one or more statements, usually towards the end of the paragraph.

Connect the body paragraphs so that your discussion flows smoothly. Use some linking words and phrases such as 'similarly' and 'on the other hand', though don't start every paragraph like this. Another strategy is to use a significant word from the last sentence of one paragraph in the first sentence of the next.

Use key terms from the topic – or synonyms for them – throughout, so the relevance of your discussion to the topic is always clear.

The conclusion ties everything together and finishes the essay. It includes strong statements that emphasise your central argument and provide a clear response to the topic.

Avoid simply restating the points made earlier in the essay – this will end on a very flat note and imply that you have run out of ideas and vocabulary. The conclusion should be a logical extension of what you have written, not just a repetition or summary of it. Writing an effective conclusion can be a challenge. Try using these tips:

- Start by linking back to the final sentence of the second-last paragraph, rather than leaping to your main contention straight away – this helps your writing to flow.
- Use synonyms and expressions with equivalent meanings to vary your vocabulary. This allows you to reinforce your line of argument without being repetitive.
- When planning your essay, think of one or two broad statements or observations about the text's wider meaning. These should be related to the topic and your overall argument. Keep them for the conclusion, since they will give you something 'new' to say but still follow logically from your discussion. The introduction will be focused on the topic, but the conclusion can present a wider view of the text.

Essay topics

1 "I felt caught like the cigarette in that contraption on her finger."
'Joe's downfall is entirely of his own making.'
Do you agree?

2 How does *Sunset Boulevard* successfully combine the genres of film noir and romance?

3 'Norma is the real victim in *Sunset Boulevard*.'
Do you agree?

4 'In order to succeed in Hollywood, the only values that really count are ambition and self-interest.'
Discuss.

5 How does the structure of the film influence the audience's response to Joe?

6 'Norma is motivated by fear more than anything else.'
Do you agree?

7 'In *Sunset Boulevard*, romantic relationships are about fantasy and illusion rather than reality.'
Discuss.

8 "Well, I sure turned into an interesting driveway."
'Joe's experience shows how easy it is to lose sight of the important things in life.'
Do you agree?

9 'Hollywood is a hierarchy.'
How does the film explore the idea of power?

10 "I'd started concocting a little plot of my own."
'The characters in *Sunset Boulevard* all make bad choices.'
Discuss.

Vocabulary for writing on *Sunset Boulevard*

Cinematography: the way in which the camera is used to capture images on film.

Circular structure: the narrative begins and ends at the same, or a similar, point.

Crosscutting: the use of cuts to shift between two scenes or events that are occurring simultaneously.

Diegesis: all the elements contained within the world of the film.

Dissolve: an editing technique where one scene briefly overlaps or 'dissolves' into the next.

Flashback/flashforward: an editing technique that shows events from the past or, alternatively, moves the plot forward to a point in the future.

Intertextuality: the deliberate referencing of other texts within a text.

Mise en scène: a French term meaning 'putting on stage', and encompassing all the visual and design elements within the frame – actors, locations, sets, background details, costumes and lighting.

Montage: a series of very short scenes or shots to convey the passing of time, sometimes set to music.

Motif: a recurring image used to link ideas and reinforce themes; adds cohesion and unity to the text.

Panning: continuous movement of the camera from side to side to shoot a panorama or keep a moving person or object in view.

Retrospective narrative: the narrator looks back on past events with the advantage of hindsight.

Voice-over: spoken commentary or narration by a character not currently seen on screen.

Zooming: the use of a zoom lens to change the focal length during a shot, creating the feeling that the camera is moving towards or away from the subject.

Analysing a sample topic

"Well, I sure turned into an interesting driveway."
'Joe's experience shows how easy it is to lose sight of the important things in life.'
Do you agree?

This topic focuses on Joe's personal trajectory and asks you to evaluate his priorities and choices. This makes a couple of assumptions, and you do not have to take either one at face value. *Has* Joe lost sight of what's important? *Is* it an easy process for him? Make your contention clear in the introduction and indicate your line of argument.

- Identify the topic quotation and look at the context in which it appears. Why does Joe say this? The quotation positions you to start with Joe's relationship with Norma. However, you must also consider the other things that happen to him.
- Identify Joe's priorities at the beginning of the film. Do these change?
- What choices does he make? Who is hurt by them? Who benefits?
- What *are* the important things in life? What does the film suggest about false values versus the importance of love, friendship, personal integrity and the merit of using one's talent?

The following plan is only one way to tackle the question. You could certainly weight this response more in Joe's favour, arguing that, although he made mistakes, he was essentially well-intentioned rather than opportunistic.

Sample introduction

> Billy Wilder's acerbic drama *Sunset Boulevard* demonstrates the ease with which a fallible man can lose his way. While Joe is in the relationship with Norma Desmond, he does lose sight of the important things. He trades love for expediency, repays loyalty and friendship with betrayal, and surrenders

his independence. Most importantly, he loses his self-respect. This happens incrementally over time, in a series of small compromises that, at first, seem relatively innocuous. Inevitably these lead to a greater capitulation. However, at the end of the text, Joe redeems himself and reclaims his integrity, albeit at great cost.

Body paragraph outline

Paragraph 1: Making it in Hollywood demands compromise and, arguably, Joe starts to lose sight of what is important as soon as he arrives there.

- Joe has come to Hollywood in the hope of making his name as a screenwriter.
- The film industry, driven by intense competition and a self-serving culture, encourages a cynical mindset.
- His principles are fluid; he lies when it suits him, and has an eye for the main chance.
- He is prepared to do whatever is required by the studios to sell his scripts: 'It's just a rehash of something that wasn't very good to begin with.'

Paragraph 2: The 'interesting driveway' offers an apparent lifeline.

- Joe is susceptible to Norma's proposition because he is financially vulnerable. He agrees to edit her script.
- He ends up prostituting himself: 'I haven't been keeping myself at all lately.'
- Equal measures of self-pity and self-contempt enable him to rationalise his position.
- Note mise en scène. Joe's new wardrobe is the tangible symbol of his loss of independence. His cheap jacket and baggy pants are replaced by a vicuña coat and formal evening wear.

Paragraph 3: Joe not only fails himself; he also fails others.

- Joe cuts himself off from his friends and shows a cavalier disregard for other people's feelings.
- He takes advantage of Artie's loyalty and good nature; he asks to sleep on his couch, but then loses contact / behaves erratically on New Year's Eve.
- Joe is unappreciative of Betty's attempts to help him; he rejects her pitch regarding 'Dark Windows'.

Paragraph 4: Falling in love is the key to Joe's redemption.

- Joe is ashamed of how he has allowed himself to be used.
- He sacrifices a future with Betty, believing she is better off without him.
- The decision to return to Dayton implies a rejection of Hollywood's values.
- He also sacrifices himself (reinforces the Salome and John the Baptist motif).

Sample conclusion

> The compromises that Joe makes in his professional life are the first steps towards moral failure. He does lose sight of important values such as self-worth and loyalty to friends. Moreover, the text shows how readily this can happen in Hollywood, where success and failure are defined purely in monetary terms. Ultimately, though, Joe's fundamental decency reasserts itself and he makes choices that are altruistic rather than selfish, principled rather than opportunistic.

SAMPLE ANSWER

"I'd started concocting a little plot of my own."
'The characters in *Sunset Boulevard* all make bad choices.'
Discuss.

Most of the characters in Billy Wilder's caustic film noir *Sunset Boulevard* make bad choices; their actions are selfish and destructive. There are several reasons why this is so, but being blinded by self-interest is a leading one. While intentions may vary from misguided to malevolent, the resultant choices are rarely wise. At the same time, if Wilder is critical of the mistakes these characters make, he is also critical of the culture that spawns them. Hollywood is a context in which, too often, narcissism and greed dictate behaviour.

Few of the characters in the text stop to consider the consequences of their behaviour, or the effect on those around them. Swept up by their own desires, they seem unable to anticipate potential pitfalls. Norma is the prime example. Her actions are driven exclusively by an egocentric insistence on her own self-importance – a dangerous legacy of her former celebrity. She acts reflexively, often on whim, sometimes on advice from her astrologer, with very little foresight or capacity to analyse a situation objectively. Norma's generosity always serves a purpose – to manipulate Joe – and if thwarted, she essentially throws a tantrum. Cutting her wrists with Joe's razor on New Year's Eve is a theatrical gesture designed to induce maximum guilt in Joe, and her histrionics culminate in his murder. Her rationale, 'No one ever leaves a star', represents the kind of psychotic hubris that could only have come out of Hollywood.

Joe's choices are similarly determined by self-interest, and hurt others as well as himself. The decision to leave his job in Dayton and try his luck in Hollywood is not a bad one in itself. However, the mise en scène in Joe's pokey one-roomed apartment and his shabby clothes confirm the unpalatable truth that ambition and talent are not necessarily enough.

Joe becomes so desperate to sell his scripts that he virtually gives up writing anything of merit. When Betty challenges him about the way in which he has compromised his talent, he frames it as a clear choice between success – albeit modest – and failure: 'That was last year. This year I'm trying to earn a living.'

Joe's 'little plot' to engineer a job for himself ghostwriting for Norma Desmond backfires badly. In becoming the former star's kept lover, Joe betrays his integrity in a way that is weak and lazy. He seems resigned to abandoning his career – 'I've given up writing altogether' – and living purely in the moment. It is Betty who reignites his ambition, with her own enthusiasm and persistence. Joe shifts from adamantly rejecting her proposal to rework 'Dark Windows', to 'playing hooky' in the evenings to collaborate on the script. This decision to start working again is an act of subconscious rebellion, an attempt to carve back some personal space from the control that Norma wields over his life.

The text shows that, at some point, people have to take responsibility for the choices they make. Of the four main characters in the text, Betty is the one with the most integrity. Nevertheless, her desire to write with Joe is also motivated by ambition and she is disinclined to take 'no' for an answer: 'I'd kind of hoped to get in on this deal.' Further, it is disingenuous to say falling in love with Joe just 'happened': Betty has been attracted to Joe from the beginning. Arguably, her decision to work with him in the intimacy of her office at night is playing with fire and, predictably, her behaviour leads to the betrayal of her fiancé.

Even choices that may seem unselfish are not necessarily wise. Joe's rejection of Betty robs her of agency. Despite her shock and hurt, she is prepared to forgive Joe – 'I haven't heard any of this' – offering him a way out when she tells him to pack his things and leave the palazzo. The camera looks up to Joe as he makes his sacrifice, suggesting that his motives are honourable, but they are based on his belief that he is no longer deserving of love. At this point, Joe feels that he has no choice at all.

On the face of it, Max's decision to turn his back on his once successful career presents an antithesis to the raw ambition that characterises Hollywood. Cecil B. DeMille's success is an intimation of the career that Max might have enjoyed; instead, he gives it all up in order to devote himself to a life of service. Disturbingly, though, Max is just as invested in the myth of Norma's stardom as she is, and his 'protection' of her goes well beyond what is altruistic or prudent. Joe tells him that they are 'not helping her any, feeding her lies and more lies'. After she kills Joe, the only way Max can shield Norma from the fallout is by pandering to her insanity even further.

Norma's world of obsessive self-delusion is a vortex into which Joe is sucked and from which he cannot escape. His sardonic voice-over cannot disguise the fact that, true to its noir conventions, *Sunset Boulevard* ends bleakly. With hindsight, nothing about Joe's death is an accident. Rather, it is the culmination of a series of damaging choices made by the key participants in the drama, which play out with tragic logic.

REFERENCES AND READING

Text

Sunset Boulevard 1950, dir. Billy Wilder, Paramount. Starring Gloria Swanson and William Holden.

References

Brogdon, W 1950, 'Sunset Boulevard', *Variety*, 19 April, https://variety.com/1950/film/reviews/sunset-boulevard-2-1200416751/

Ebert, R 1999, 'Sunset Boulevard', *Roger Ebert*, 27 June, https://www.rogerebert.com/reviews/great-movie-sunset-boulevard-1950

Eggert, B 2016, 'Sunset Blvd', *Deep Focus Review*, 6 March, https://deepfocusreview.com/definitives/sunset-blvd/

Hutchinson, P 2016, '*Sunset Boulevard*: what Billy Wilder's satire really tells us about Hollywood', *The Guardian*, 1 August, https://www.theguardian.com/film/2016/aug/01/sunset-boulevard-what-billy-wilders-satire-really-tells-us-about-hollywood

Joudrey, T 2020, '*Sunset Boulevard* at 70: we're all Norma Desmond now', *The Guardian*, 4 August, https://www.theguardian.com/film/2020/aug/04/sunset-boulevard-at-70-were-all-norma-desmond-now

Mikulec, S n.d., '*Sunset Boulevard*: Billy Wilder and Charles Brackett's Sobering Exposure of the Dark Side of Hollywood', *Cinephilia & Beyond*, https://cinephiliabeyond.org/sunset-boulevard-billy-wilder-charles-bracketts-sobering-exposure-dark-side-hollywood/

Pryor, TM 1950, 'The Screen: Inner Workings of Filmdom', *The New York Times*, 11 August, https://archive.nytimes.com/www.nytimes.com/books/98/12/27/specials/wilder-sunset.html

Staggs, S 2002, *Close-Up on Sunset Boulevard: Billy Wilder, Norma Desmond, and the Dark Hollywood Dream*, St Martin's Press, New York.

THR staff 1950, '*Sunset Boulevard*: THR's 1950 Review', *The Hollywood Reporter*, 17 April, https://www.hollywoodreporter.com/movies/movie-news/sunset-boulevard-review-movie-1950-1235172387

Further reading

Sikov, E 2017, *On Sunset Boulevard: The Life and Times of Billy Wilder*, University Press of Mississippi, Jackson.

'The Production Code of 1930', University of North Dakota, www.und.edu/instruct/cjacobs/ProductionCode.htm

Note: As part of the study of *Sunset Boulevard*, it would be worthwhile for students to watch some of Billy Wilder's other great films, especially the noir classics *Double Indemnity* (1944) and *The Lost Weekend* (1945).